Heaven's Design

A Treasure Chest Of Insights To Help You
Build Your Marriage From God's Perspective.

By:

ROBB D. THOMPSON

Heaven's Design
ISBN 1-889723-70-3
Copyright © 2006 by Robb Thompson
Family Harvest Church
18500 92nd Ave.
Tinley Park, Illinois 60487

Collaborative Development: Karen B. Jahn, Dr. Dennis D. Sempebwa
Editing: Dr. Dennis D. Sempebwa, Karen B. Jahn
Proofreading: Donna Friend
Design: Amanda Fico

Contents

Introduction

The task I am about to undertake is dangerous at best. It is filled with opinions, dreams, and nightmares — psychological opinions and dreams of what could be and nightmares of what should have been, but isn't. This journey is not for the fainthearted but for the eternally committed. For some, these words will be teeming with the hope of a future divinely designed. For others, it will be a revealing story of dreams gone awry. Regardless of our personal circumstances, we all enter marriage with the expectation that it will be wonderful. In this book, the first of a three-book series, I hope to equip you with the tools you need to turn those hopeful expectations into realities.

This is not an easy subject to teach, because marriage itself can be very difficult. If you're married, you know how true that is! However, achieving an excellent marriage relationship would be very simple if we all entered into it with the right heart. We just have to be determined to stay open and loving toward each other and to do what God has called us to do as husbands or wives, respectively. Problems only arise when we decide that we *don't* want to live as we were designed to live within our marriage relationships. Sounds simple, doesn't it? Then why is it that so many couples, including Christians, just don't make it?

I want to share with you what the Scriptures have to say about our marriages and our respective positions in the home. This is so important, because most of us are confused about how to build a good marriage. We're not really sure what it means to be a Godly husband or wife. We've heard so many different opinions in the world about the way marriage is supposed to work. Sadly, we often turn to these worldly opinions instead of turning to God's Word.

I believe that the root problem behind most of the issues couples face is a spiritual one. And using psychology to fix spiritual problems is just not possible. Spiritual problems demand spiritual solutions. You see, Christians who allow themselves to get dragged into the realm of psychology often latch on to opinions that give them an excuse for getting their own way. They read all kinds of books and magazine articles on how to make their marriages better, but they fail to study the Bible to discover what God says about the subject. As a result, they embrace wrong ideas that keep them from becoming what God designed for them to be in their relationship with their spouse. People who follow this path of deception often see their marriages destroyed for lack of true knowledge. The Bible says in the book of Hosea, chapter four and verse six that *"My people are destroyed for lack of knowledge…"*

Through the years, I've noticed that this problem has encroached upon the church at large. We have actually become more psychological than spiritual in our approach to marriage. Pastors often become little more than glorified marriage counselors, as they try to help couples keep their marriages together using psychological principles.

But psychology alone cannot solve marital difficulties. The real answer lies in taking a closer look at the "Owner's Manual for Marriage" — the Word of God — and making the decision to build an excellent marriage *God's* way.

Personally, I'm not interested in what others think about marriage. I'm also not interested in what I think about marriage. I'm only interested in *what God thinks* about it. For more than a quarter of a century, I've been willing to give up my opinions and to live, to the best of my ability, according to God's opinions regarding the issues of life. I'm not saying it's always easy to do that, especially in the arena of marriage. But the rewards of making God's perspective *my* perspective have always been well worth the price of obedience.

You will need to adopt this same attitude, if you want to work toward a healthy, happy marriage. Whether you're a husband or a wife, God has provided instructions in His Word that will bring you to a place of fulfillment in your marriage, beyond anything you've ever imagined. But you will only find that place of fulfillment if you work on your marriage *His* way — even when it's hard to swallow the truth.

The way God says marriage is supposed to work is definitely *not* the same as what the world says. In fact, God's perspective and the world's perspective have been on opposite sides of the spectrum ever since the fall of man. This is true concerning all arenas of life, but especially marriage.

Whether or not you realize it, each of us spends our entire married life trying to make something right that went wrong long ago in the Garden of Eden. But like everything else, mankind cannot make marriages right by using natural reasoning. We must discover what God says about marriage and then be willing to change to His way of doing things.

As you go through this journey of discovery, don't allow yourself to become offended by the Word of God. Psalm 119:165 (KJV) says, *"Great peace have they which love thy law: and nothing shall offend them."* Change isn't always easy, but as you determine to receive the instruction of wisdom (Proverbs 1:3) and obey God's pattern concerning marriage, your life will be all the better for it.

In my experience as a leader, I meet so many people who *are* married but are desperately trying to get out; at the same time, I meet unmarried people whose *only focus* is finding the right person and building a lifetime marriage relationship. If we could only get these two groups to switch their focuses, everything would work out a lot better, right?!

The reason many married couples don't want to be married is that they are unwilling to change. In fact, I believe the greatest problem a marriage can face is when each partner blames *the other* for what he or she is not receiving, yet refuses to *give* the very thing they want to receive.

The truth is that God's Word will work in a marriage *only* if both parties are willing to change. When only one person starts obeying the Word in the marriage relationship, the other spouse often begins to take advantage of what he or she perceives as weakness in the other marriage partner. Yet the very opposite is true: Our present culture may call this humility *weakness*, but God calls it *strength*.

You can't have a healthy marriage without being willing to change. It just isn't possible. As long as you live in this flawed world, your marriage will never be perfect. But you can make it *excellent*, if you and your spouse are willing to do it God's way, no matter what.

As you read *Heaven's Design*, keep this in mind: When you go to God's Word, stop looking for what it says about your spouse; look for how it speaks to you about *you*. Whenever you go to the Word, you are to receive its instruction for yourself, not for someone else. You are to learn what is *your* responsibility before God and then do what His Word tells you to do.

We should never use God's Word to prove to our mate where he or she is wrong; that will only make matters worse. Instead, we need to ingest the Word into ourselves, so we can become everything God has called *us* to be in our marriage.

I can tell you from experience that you can't make your spouse change; nor can your spouse make you change. When each of you approaches the marriage gate, you approach it as individuals with specific instructions from God, not from each other.

I don't go to the Word to find out what my wife is supposed to do. I go so I can learn what *I* am supposed to do, as a husband in the Lord. And I don't just learn what the Word says. I know that I will be changed only by actually *doing* the Word, not by simply *hearing* it.

Of course, that doesn't mean I haven't made mistakes in my marriage. In this marriage series, I will tell you some things about myself that might not sound very complimentary. But that's all right. I don't have a problem with being open and sharing my shortcomings with you. I am very weary of Christians who hide all their problems in their homes and then go to church pretending they have it all together in their spiritual walk.

I understand that even having a gift to teach on this subject — or on any other subject in the Bible, for that matter — doesn't mean I have a gift to *live* it. I have to go through the same struggles and learn the same hard lessons as everyone else. The truth is, we're all on the same escalator of learning in this area of life. Some of us may be a little higher on that escalator, but we all have a long way to go!

So let me ask you this right up front: *Do you like where your marriage is right now?* If you don't, here's one more question for you: *When was the last time you did something for your marriage?*

Things don't just happen. Maybe you got married thinking your marriage would work out just because it would work out. But think about it for a moment. You have to go to school to learn geography. Wouldn't you say that your marriage is more important than geography?

So stay with me as I present a short course on building an excellent marriage — tuition-free and complete with a teacher who has taken the course ahead of you! All you need to get started is this book, a Bible — and a strong willingness to *change* into the husband or wife God called you to be!

Dr. Robert Daniels Thompson

CHAPTER 1

In The Beginning

God created marriage to be an expression of Himself. It is interesting, however, that when a man and a woman come together in holy matrimony, it often isn't very long at all before the marriage looks like it has nothing to do with God!

How did we become so confused about the concept of marriage, and how can we fix the problem? To answer this question, we have to go back to the very beginning of the human race.

A Perfect Institution

When God created marriage, He created it absolutely perfect. It was without flaw until the day the first man and woman disobeyed God's command and sinned. At that moment, everything on this earth got "out of sync" — including the holy institution of marriage. Since then, mankind has been attempting to make right what went wrong so long ago in the Garden of Eden.

In their search for answers, desperate couples run to society for answers. They immediately hit walls, because frankly, society has no answers. In today's culture, abnormal has become the new "normal." *Dysfunction* is now the way most marriages *function*! I'm so thankful that God has provided the way, through His Word, for us to get back in sync with His original design for marriage.

Let's read Genesis 2:

> *And the Lord God formed man of the dust of the ground, and breathed into his nostrils the breath of life; and man became a living being.*
>
> *The Lord God planted a garden eastward in Eden, and there He put the man whom He had formed.*
>
> *Then the Lord God took the man and put him in the Garden of Eden to tend and keep it. And the Lord God commanded the man, saying, "Of every tree of the garden you may freely eat; but of the tree of the knowledge of good and evil you shall not eat, for in the day that you eat of it you shall surely die."*
>
> *And the Lord God said, "It is not good that man should be alone; I will make him a helper comparable to him."*
>
> Genesis 2:7-8,15-18

In the beginning, God not only fathered Adam, but He

personally mentored him. Adam was actually instructed as a student of the one Teacher who never makes a mistake and is perfect in all His ways. The first man and his Creator enjoyed a wonderful, intimate relationship, in which both of them continually knew their respective roles.

However, God perceived that it was not good for the man to be without a helper comparable to himself. So, the first woman was introduced into the picture:

> *So Adam gave names to all cattle, to the birds of the air, and to every beast of the field. But for Adam there was not found a helper comparable to him.*
>
> *And the Lord God caused a deep sleep to fall on Adam, and he slept; and He took one of his ribs, and closed up the flesh in its place.*
>
> *Then the rib, which the Lord God had taken from man, He made into a woman, and He brought her to the man.*
>
> Genesis 2:20-22

I want to point out a central truth from this passage of Scripture that will help you understand a common dilemma that countless married couples have experienced through the ages.

If you are a wife like most women, you see characteristics that frustrate you in the man God sent into your life. Your husband doesn't think like you think, and that bothers you greatly. But there is a good reason why he doesn't think or act like you. Notice what verse 21 says: After causing a deep sleep to come upon Adam, God took out one of his ribs, and from that rib He formed a woman. That means God *took out of* (or removed from) man everything that makes you a woman!

That's exactly why your husband needs you so much. You are the one who *feels*. Even if you were taught to hold down your emotions, your entire psyche still runs by emotion; his doesn't. Your response to outside stimulation is much different. You're easily touched by hardships that other people go through; he isn't. He usually has to be shown a problem that needs to be solved before he even gets involved or engages. In fact, he might look somewhat self-centered. But the truth is that he's just a little dull in the areas where you're strong!

He Needs Her

I believe that a man needs a woman much more than a woman needs a man. Women have the thoughtfulness, tenderness, and consideration of other people's feelings that he doesn't think much about. He just wants to bulldoze through life without distraction. But whenever he gets too busy trudging through the mountains and boring holes in the valleys, his wife is there to say, "Wait a second — let's stop and smell the roses for a minute." That's why God gave her as a gift to him — so he wouldn't be all work, with no thought for the other things that really matter in life.

God designed marriage this way on purpose. He took the woman out of the man so that the gaps in man's emotional side — the missing elements that perhaps cause him to be warm and loving—could be filled in by the woman God gives him. Without her, the man is not complete.

It's important to understand this concept, wives. Your husband isn't like you, and he'll never be like you. He isn't as pretty as you, and he doesn't smell as good as you do—and he doesn't care if he does. Remember: He was made from the dirt!

> A WISE MAN *Discovers* THAT HE NEEDS HIS WIFE MORE THAN SHE NEEDS HIM.

We men are incomplete without our wives. We need them, even though their complexities frustrate us! *We will never perfectly understand our wives, because the qualities they have inside of them are the very qualities we lack.*

You need her, husbands. God has given her to make you a more complete person and to be your complement. She is to be a helper, one who is called alongside of you to be the kind of asset and treasure that no one else in life could ever be.

One Flesh

That's why the Bible says *the two shall become one flesh.*

And Adam said: "This is now bone of my bones and flesh of my flesh; she shall be called Woman, because she was taken out of Man." Therefore a man shall leave his father and mother and be joined to his wife, and they shall become one flesh.

Genesis 2:23-24

13

God took woman out of man and then gave her back to him so the two could become one. With that divine act, the institution of marriage was created. One became two; then two became one.

Nothing was added to woman that didn't come from the man. Even her soul and spirit were found in the man, for God breathed the breath of life into man, not woman, and then formed woman out of man (Genesis 2:7, 22).

In the beginning, the two were a single unit, completely inseparable. They had the same name, for God saw them as one: *"Male and female created He them; and blessed them, and **called their name Adam**, in the day when they were created"* (Genesis 5:2 KJV). Isn't that fascinating?

Then came the day when the woman said, "I'm not going to walk the way of agreement any longer." (Keep in mind that at this time, the woman had as much authority as the man and was supposed to use that authority to walk side by side with Adam.) Suddenly the one became two once more, as sin drove them apart. Since then, husbands and wives have had to struggle to become one again.

Notice that verse 24 says, *"a man shall leave his father and mother and be joined to his wife."* Husbands, the Bible tells you right here that your wife must always be more important to you than your parents. Her thoughts, desires, and opinions must mean more to you than anything your parents might say.

So if your parents have ever come between you and your

wife, you need to explain to them that those days are over. Tell them, "Mom and Dad, I love and respect you, but I'm not ten years old anymore. I'm responsible for someone else, so please let us make our own decisions." Leaving one's parents and cleaving to one's spouse is all a part of "the two becoming one."

In Genesis 3:1-6, we see that things began to go wrong in that first marriage when the serpent came to beguile and deceive the woman, and the man failed to take his place as her protector.

> Now the serpent was more cunning than any beast of the field, which the Lord God had made. And he said to the woman, "Has God indeed said, 'You shall not eat of every tree of the garden'?"
>
> And the woman said to the serpent, "We may eat the fruit of the trees of the garden; but of the fruit of the tree which is in the midst of the garden, God has said, 'You shall not eat it, nor shall you touch it, lest you die.'"
>
> Then the serpent said to the woman, "You will not surely die. For God knows that in the day you eat of it your eyes will be opened, and you will be like God, knowing good and evil."
>
> So when the woman saw that the tree was good for food, that it was pleasant to the eyes, and a tree desirable to make one wise, she took of its fruit and ate. She also gave to her husband with her, and he ate.
>
> Genesis 3:1-6

☞ *Relinquished Leadership* ☜

God created perfection; but perfection was perverted on that dreadful day when Adam failed to lead and protect his wife. She was lured into deception by the enemy. Adam allowed his own authority to be overthrown in his own domain.

A MAN MUST NEVER ALLOW HIS DIVINE *Responsibilities* TO BE OVERTHROWN FOR THE SAKE OF COUNTERFEIT HARMONY.

The Bible says the man was right there with the woman, as she was tempted by the enemy. Adam knew the right answers to the serpent's questions, but he didn't do anything about it. When he heard his wife incorrectly quote the Lord to the serpent, he didn't correct her or help her to understand what God had really said. Instead, Adam tried to maintain harmony with his wife, allowing his authority to be overthrown (as he followed his wife's lead and took a bite of the forbidden fruit).

Adam's plan backfired, however, achieving nothing more than counterfeit harmony and a world of sorrow. Why? *Because peace can never be maintained by forfeiture of one's authority.*

Up until that time, there was absolutely no reason for anyone to vie for control. But from that moment forward, the fight was on! For the first time, a separation existed between husband and wife. Her name was no longer "Woman," the one who came from Man; now she was called "Eve," mother of all living. In other words, she went from being "The Queen of Life" to "Just the Mother of My Kids!"

At that moment, perfection in the first marriage died. The very institution God had created to bring joy and fulfillment to man and woman would now be a source of heartache as well. Adam would have a problem bringing forth fruit from the ground, and Eve would have a problem bearing her children. No longer would marriage be happy and trouble-free. No longer could husband and wife live easily together as intimate lovers and friends. Suddenly they both faced *problems*. The struggle for control had begun, and that struggle changed everything.

Although I'm certain God knew this was going to happen, I don't think for a moment that He desired it. God wanted you and me to live in the Garden today as loyal subjects to His Kingdom, never knowing one day, one moment, or even *one second* of sin, nor what it means to be estranged from Him. But God refused to violate the free will He gave man. Adam and Eve were free to choose either disobedience or obedience and then to suffer the consequences or enjoy the rewards of their choices.

He Shall Rule Over Thee

In verse 16, the Lord pronounced one of the most significant consequences of disobedience when He said to Eve, "...*Your desire shall be for your husband, and he shall rule over*

17

you." In other words, God said to the woman, "Your desire shall be to rule over your husband; but I have commanded him to rule over you."

Wives, God never called you to rule over your husband. The greatest fight you will ever have in your life is the fight for control. You want to be in charge. You desire to be the one who decides how to deal with a particular situation. But realize this: You didn't get that desire for control on your own; you were born with it. Eve gave it to you long ago, when she decided that the word of her husband was not as preeminent as the word of the devil.

TO ENJOY *Harmony,* YOU MUST FIRST UNDERSTAND DIVINE AUTHORITY.

You may say, "That's not true about me, Robb. I don't want to be in charge." You need to look in the mirror and be honest with yourself. You probably don't try to take control in your marriage with brute force. You may try to get your way by arguing or manipulating; you may even do it with sweetness. But one way or another, you find yourself trying to control situations in order to have things go the way *you* want them to go.

Think about it, wives — do you ever turn a cold shoulder, argue, or let the tears flow when you don't get your way? If the answer is yes, just know that you are dealing with a common problem in marriage: You desire to rule. But God hasn't called you to rule in your marriage.

Please understand where I'm coming from here. I love women! I don't believe God ever made an ugly one. I think women are awesome. But at the same time, the Bible says that since the fall of man, women have been born with a flaw — that is, their need to control.

Now let's look at what God said to Adam in Genesis 3:17:

> "...Because you have heeded the voice of your wife, and have eaten from the tree of which I commanded you, saying, 'You shall not eat of it': cursed is the ground for your sake; in toil you shall eat of it all the days of your life."

The word *heed* (the KJV says *hearken*) means not only to listen to someone, but also to "take to heart" what he says and *to obey* him. Notice that God *didn't* tell Adam, "Because you have listened to and obeyed the devil, the earth is cursed for your sake." God told him, "The earth is cursed because you have listened to and obeyed the voice of your *wife*."

That doesn't mean a wife adds no value to a husband's thoughts and decisions, because she does. She has a valuable perspective that the husband doesn't have. She thinks thoughts that he doesn't think. She understands things that he doesn't understand. And in most cases, she is more spiritual than he is. As the influencer behind the leader, she can often stand back and make a better judgment in any given situation. But here's the point: *Leading the family is not what God has called her to do.*

God didn't call the wife to rule over the husband. So

whenever she tries to take control in the marriage relationship, big problems always result.

The Great Disconnect

Let's look at one of the problems that resulted after Eve took the lead. Instead of the beautiful relationship God had created between man and woman, fear and insecurity now ruled. Before they disobeyed, they walked together in the Garden, naked and not ashamed (Genesis 2:25). Certainly this refers to physical nakedness, but that word *naked* also carries the meaning of *emotional nakedness or transparency*.

Before the fall of man, the first man and woman had no walls built between them. Nothing prevented them from enjoying the deepest fellowship with one another. No wrong attitudes hindered them from being open and loving with one another. They were always excited and blessed to be in each other's presence. They never wanted to slip away from one another, because they weren't ashamed of each other in any way.

WALLS THAT DIVIDE A *Marriage* ARE THOSE THAT MUST NEVER BE GIVEN A BUILDING PERMIT.

Think about your own marriage for a moment. What are some of the biggest problems you and your spouse face? More than likely, your list includes the fact that you really can't be *completely open* with one another.

Now, you may always be truthful, but that doesn't mean you're always transparent. You know you can't lie, so you tell the truth. But at the same time, you're not always open with your spouse. Why not? Because, in one way or another, you fear the outcome. You don't want to deal with what may happen if you say what you really think.

"Well, I don't tell my husband everything I do because I know he'll blow up about the situation if I do."

Well, if you know your husband would blow up about it, why do you do it?

"Well, yes, but he's really wrong in how he reacts to this situation."

Then you need to pick the right time for you and him to go to war! However, let me give you a tip: The right time is probably *not* during the most important football game of the season!

The truth is, some couples live their entire married lives together and never truly communicate with each other. Perhaps at some point early in their marriage, one spouse reacted with anger when the other finally became transparent and told the truth; as a result, the spouse who attempted to be open and transparent decided never to do it again.

Some marriage partners go years without ever being open with each other, until one of them finally decides, *"I'm not taking this anymore!"* Suddenly the marriage begins to fragment and fall apart, and they wonder what just happened — all because both spouses aren't communicating. They are afraid of what might happen if they do, and they ignore what most certainly *will* happen if they don't!

Fig Leaves

The fear and insecurity that keeps spouses from being open with each other originated way back in the Garden of Eden. With disobedience came man's first taste of shame: *"Then the eyes of both of them were opened, and they knew that they were naked; and they sewed fig leaves together and made themselves coverings"* (Genesis 3:7).

When Adam and Eve sewed those fig leaves together to make coverings for themselves, they were not only hiding from God, but also from one another. The communication lines went down. They were no longer interested in revealing themselves to one another. Total transparency became too much of a risk. So they sewed fig leaves together in an attempt to restore their self-esteem and prove that everything was fine and wonderful.

We do the same thing in our marriages today with our own versions of "fig leaves." Each one of our fig leaves has a name on it, such as "fear," "insecurity," and "low self-esteem." We link all these "leaves" together to put on a front, because we don't want anyone, including our spouse, to see who we really are. Pretending on the outside that everything is wonderful, we hide behind our fig leaves, knowing in our hearts that everything is definitely not wonderful. But God wants us to face the truth about ourselves, so we can begin to take off those fig leaves, one by one, and become transparent with our spouse.

After that fateful moment when man failed to protect his wife, both man and woman began to protect themselves. (This is a very important point to keep in mind, for it permeates all of our thinking.) Suddenly they were ashamed of who they were. They could no longer be open with each other. They didn't want to tell each other the truth anymore. The bliss and the wonder of their time spent together turned to horror in a single moment.

The Blame Game

Then the Lord came walking in the Garden in the cool of the day and called, "Adam, where are you?" There was no reply.

The Lord called out again, "Adam, where are you?" Again there was no reply, but this time Adam reluctantly came out of his hiding place wearing the covering he made with the fig leaves.

God asked him, "Where have you been, Adam?"

Adam timidly replied, "Well, I heard You walking in the Garden in the cool of the day and was afraid, because I was naked."

"Who told you that you were naked? Adam, have you been eating of the tree I commanded you to avoid?"

"It was the woman You gave me who made me do it, Lord!"

Right there the blame game began. Right there it became someone else's fault for life.

So what was God's original purpose in giving woman to man? We find the answer in Genesis 2:18: *"And the Lord God said, 'It is not good that man should be alone; I will make him a helper comparable to him.'"*

Notice that God didn't make Adam for Eve; rather, He made Eve for Adam. She was sent to be a helper to him because after Adam named all the animals of the earth, all the birds of the air, and all the fish of the sea, *"...for Adam there was not found a helper comparable to [or fit for] him"* (v. 20).

∾ Problem Solvers ∾

Remember this: *God created everything to solve a problem.* He gave you every good thing in your life to solve some sort of problem. You have a coat to solve the problem of feeling cold when you go outside. You have a can opener because cans are in your cupboard that need to be opened.

Well, in marriage, you and your spouse have been chosen by God to solve problems for each other. You certainly don't get married because you need a new father or a new mother. You get married because there is one who has been called by God to come alongside you and be something to you that no one else in life could ever be. With that special person, you can finally be naked, open, and transparent instead of clothed with a "fig leaf façade" of self-protection and lies. However, the moment you stop looking for ways to make your spouse's life better, you become a *problem-creator* instead of a *problem-solver*.

There was a time when my wife, Linda, resisted the idea of being in the ministry. Neither of us was even saved when we got married, so Linda never expected the many demands of full-time ministry to become the focus of our lives. It wasn't what she had signed up for, and for a long time she didn't want any part of it.

In fact, while everyone on the outside was saying what a great guy I was, Linda was having a difficult time even liking me! She saw me as this person who didn't have time to love her. I was too busy laying down my life for everyone else. I didn't have time to do all the things she thought I should do for her as her husband.

> YOU ARE *Celebrated* FOR THE PROBLEMS YOU SOLVE, AND REJECTED FOR THOSE YOU CREATE.

This issue almost drowned Linda. She was dwelling on all the things she thought I should be doing for *her* instead of the things she should have been doing to help *me*. But God didn't call me to be Linda's helper. God called her to be *my* helper.

HEAVEN'S DESIGN

Thank God, Linda eventually came around to accepting God's call on our lives. Today there is no one in our ministry who is a harder worker than she is!

Wives, don't be a problem-creator who does nothing but sit around the house, waiting for your husband to come home and meet your needs. Make the decision that you're going to become a problem-solver instead of a problem-creator for your husband. For instance, if you don't have small children to take care of at home, you might consider finding a valuable service organization in which to volunteer, so someone else can have an easier time in life.

Of course, you shouldn't be so busy that you can't maintain a clean and well-ordered home. Certainly you are not to offer your service to God while leaving your house in a mess. But after all, you can only clean your house so much. The point I'm making is this: Avoid becoming a problem to your husband by depending too much on him for your fulfillment in life. You need to find your fulfillment in Christ Jesus; then you will be prepared to *give* to your husband, instead of always needing to *receive* from him.

God created the first man to solve a problem for Himself — a fellowship problem. He created the first woman to solve a problem for the man — a companionship problem. Marriage was created to be *an answer* to problems, not to *become* a problem.

The element that caused strife and heartache in the first marriage is the same element that causes upheaval in today's marriages — disobedience to God's commands. As you and your spouse commit to turn your backs on disobedience and make the decision to become doers of God's Word, you will see your marriage relationship grow and flourish.

CHAPTER PRINCIPLES

- A wise man discovers that he needs his wife more than she needs him.

- A man must never allow his divine responsibilities to be overthrown for the sake of counterfeit harmony.

- To enjoy harmony, you must first understand divine authority.

- Walls that divide a marriage are those that must never be given a building permit.

- You are celebrated for the problems you solve and rejected for those you create.

Chapter 2

Taking Care of Business

All married couples were created to solve a problem in their marriage relationship. That means they each must discover the answers to these questions: *"What is my assignment in this marriage? How do I fulfill that assignment?"*

ᴄ Your Pre-assigned Role ᴄ

If a husband and wife don't understand their God-given assignments in their marriage, they will always strive with each other for position and control. Their lives become a perpetual wrestling match to find out who will be the one to run the marriage. As a result, the couple never really enjoys their relationship.

The only time things begin to go right for you in your marriage is when you and your spouse understand and accept

your respective roles. If you don't know what position you are
to fill, you are always hindered by the ever-present "wrestling
match" of wills.

NEVER TAKE
Authority
OVER SOMETHING FOR
WHICH HEAVEN HAS
NOT MADE YOU
RESPONSIBLE.

Let me clarify this for you. In every
relationship, you hold a position. It
is important to ask what that position is, and stay with it. You must
never attempt to displace another
person's position.

We can see where King Saul made that
mistake in his life. Before Saul became a king, he
was a humble man and didn't take for granted his relationships
with his superiors. One day his father sent him and a friend out
to look for some donkeys that wandered off and were lost (see
1 Samuel 9). For three days, the two young men looked for the
donkeys without success. Then suddenly Saul's friend said, "I
know how we can find them. There is a man of God we can
visit. He will tell us where the donkeys are."

But Saul respected the position of God's prophet and
protested, "I can't go to the prophet. I don't have a gift to
bring." Saul refused to treat the man of God lightly.

Saul's friend said, "Well, I have a piece of silver we can
give the prophet."

Saul replied, "Okay, then we can go."

So they went to Samuel the prophet, who said, "The donkeys have been found, and your father is wondering about

you. Stay one more day, and then you can go home." Then Samuel anointed Saul as king right there on the spot.

Later Samuel told King Saul: "...*You were once small in your own eyes...*" (1 Samuel 15:17, NIV). Notice Samuel talked about Saul's humility in the past tense, because Saul's character gradually deteriorated after he became king. The day came when he attempted to displace Samuel's position as a prophet by offering his own burnt sacrifice to the Lord (1 Samuel 13:3-14). By trying to change his position from king to prophet in that situation, Saul showed disrespect for the prophet's position. This was one of the reasons Saul lost his kingdom. God was sorry He made Saul the king, because he tried to assume a position God never called him to fill.

❧ Role Displacement ❧

In the same way, you are never to change positions in your marriage relationship, whether you are the husband or the wife. Never allow yourself to take authority over a position for which God has not made you responsible; otherwise, you cause big problems in your marriage.

If Linda doesn't do what she is supposed to do as my wife, I cannot displace her by assuming her position. Nor can she displace me if I fail to take my proper place as the husband. My wife didn't assign me to the husband's position; God did. Therefore, *I answer to Him*, not her, for how well I perform in the position to which God called me in my marriage.

Now, there are some areas in the home in which I let Linda lead. I like to do that whenever I can, because I am called to lead in so many other areas of my life. So I'll say, "Honey, I must lead in the areas for which God has made me responsible. But in the arenas where I don't have to make the decisions, it's okay with me if you take the lead."

"What do you want to eat for dinner, Robb?"

"Whatever you decide, honey."

"Do you want to go out for dinner?"

"It doesn't matter to me."

"Do you want to go to this place on our vacation?"

"I don't care, Baby."

Never take your spouse so much for granted that you bypass his or her position in your life. Allow me to illustrate what I mean by this.

A husband might say, "Oh, it will be fine if I do this. My wife won't mind if I don't let her know." Or a wife will say, "Oh, my husband doesn't really care about this issue, so I'll just make the decision myself." But did that husband or wife attempt to find out their spouse's desires? For instance, maybe the husband *does care* about that particular issue but stays quiet about it because he doesn't want to get into an argument with his wife. In any case, bypassing the spouse's position is always a demonstration of disrespect.

Husbands, I want to address you for a moment. The day

you stop leading is the day you attempt to take your wife's position in your marriage. If you don't get back in your own position, you will lose the blessings God has for you in the marriage.

Respect FOR ANOTHER'S RESPONSIBILITIES OPENS THE RARELY OPENED DOOR OF NEEDED APPRECIATION.

When a husband stops taking the initiative in his home, he opens the door for his wife to take a position to which God hasn't called her. He and his wife can only become all God wants them both to be in the marriage when *the husband* assumes his role as leader inside his home.

But let me warn you, husbands—you must have scriptural references for everything you do, because your wife *will* challenge you on your decisions. Does she want to? No. Can she stop doing it? Yes, when she *recognizes your position* in the marriage and willingly learns to follow your leadership. Until then, she will always attempt a peaceful takeover of the home.

The Law Of Recognition

What does this mean? It's called the *law of recognition*, and it works every time. Just look at David's life. Even when it looked like David was going down for the third count — when he was running for his life from King Saul — David still obtained the throne. Why? Because he always recognized and respected the position of the king. On the other hand, Saul *didn't* recognize the position of the prophet of God, and he lost the throne.

Remember the two thieves who were crucified with Jesus? One thief didn't recognize who Jesus was and began to mock Him. That thief died and went to hell. The other thief recognized Jesus' position as the Son of God, and Jesus told him, "...*Today you will be with Me in Paradise*" (Luke 23:43).

The law of recognition also works in the arena of marriage. Wives, you need to recognize the man's position of leadership in the home. And, husbands, you need to recognize the woman God sent for you to love, because the way you love her is reflective of the way you love God.

I recognize and respect my wife's position before God. That means I allow her to be free. I don't try to answer her part of the question. In fact, I'm more excited about her and who she is than I am about myself!

Look at the case of Nabal and his wife Abigail (*see* 1 Samuel 25). It was because of Abigail that David didn't kill Nabal when Nabal displayed great disrespect toward David and his men. However, because Nabal didn't recognize the value of Abigail, he later lost his life. David, on the other hand, recognized Abigail's value, and he eventually married her.

A man like Nabal doesn't recognize his wife's value. He's mean and insensitive to her, always browbeating and nagging her about what he thinks she did wrong. Something has to change in a marriage like that, or that husband will lose his treasure — the wife God gave him.

So how can you know how well you're doing at filling your position in your marriage? Well, if you're a wife, I recommend that you *don't* inquire of another woman. She'll just say, "I can't understand why your husband doesn't appreciate you! He should, because you're doing such a great job as a wife!" Instead of going to another woman, ask a man whom you respect as a good, conscientious husband to give you the definition of a good wife.

And, husbands, if you want to know what a woman considers to be a good husband, don't ask your buddy! Your friend will only cheer you on. Instead, talk to a woman whom you consider to be wise and knowledgeable on the subject.

Answerable To God

Ultimately, however, it is God who decides if you are a good husband or a good wife. Linda doesn't define for me what a husband is supposed to be; God does. In the same way, God is the One who defines for her what is a good wife. Therefore, we are each answerable to God *for how we please Him* in our respective marriage roles. Our individual accountability before God is always to be the deciding factor that controls the type of husband I am or the type of wife she is.

The biggest challenge you will ever face in your marriage

A HEALTHY
HOME BEGINS WITH
Responsibility
COUPLED WITH PERSONAL
ACCOUNTABILITY, IN
ORDER TO MAINTAIN
PROPER BALANCE.

is that of taking the position God gave you. God made you in a particular way, and your life will only work well as you fill the position God created you to fill. The only way you and your spouse will ever be happy is for both of you to operate in your marriage the way God said to do it.

When God told me to love Linda, I determined to *love* her with all my heart. I have no regrets in the way I've treated my wife, except for one: Although I take my position in my marriage very seriously, at times I don't think I have been serious enough about it.

I know what I need to do for my wife every day, and I always do more than she could ever ask me to do. At the same time, I expect my wife to do the Word of God in her life. I shouldn't have to talk her into obeying the Word; and she shouldn't have to talk me into loving her. I can't fix something in her life just by telling her to fix it, and she can't do that for me either. When I become accountable to God, my wife never has to come and adjust me. Each of us is personally accountable to God and His Word for our attitudes, words, and actions in the marriage.

≈ *Mind Your Own Business* ≈

First Thessalonians 4:11 tells me, "*...aspire to lead a quiet life, to mind your own business...*" Whether or not I obey that scripture has nothing to do with my spouse's posture or behavior. I am supposed to mind *my* own business — what *I* am responsible for in the marriage — not what my spouse is responsible for.

So what does that mean, in practical application? Well, for one thing, when your spouse attempts to correct you over an issue, your response should never be "Yeah, but you're like that, too" or "What about the things *you* do wrong?" Our spouse is not the subject of discussion at that particular moment! When this occurs, we must listen and take responsibility for what *we* need to change.

Husbands commit to going before God every day and asking, "Father, what do You require of me as a husband? What can I do to better love my wife?" It's actually very simple to be a good husband, although if you look around, you won't find many men making the effort. All husbands should focus on what *they* should do to make their marriage exceptional, instead of what their wives should do.

Wives, it's also a simple thing to learn how to be an understanding wife. Just go to God every day and ask, "What can I do to bless my husband today, Lord? How do I make this the greatest day of his life?" Soon you'll have a happy husband wondering, "*My Lord, what happened to my wife?*"

That's so much better than spending all your time complaining, *"My husband never does what I want him to do."* After all, God never instructed your husband to please you just because *you* want it; God told him to *obey His Word.*

Yes, God expects your husband to obey the Word regardless of your behavior. However, the law of sowing and reaping is an unwavering factor in every relationship. Don't be surprised if your husband fails to treat you the way you desire to be treated, if you haven't first done what God tells you to do.

"Yes, but what about *his* responsibilities toward *me?*"

Wives, as you fulfill your divine responsibilities, just keep praying for your husband and trust God to work out everything according to His purpose in your home.

Remember — marriage is not supposed to be a series of fingers pointing in the other direction. The only finger pointing should be at *yourself* as you look in the mirror! Don't worry about whether or not your spouse does the Word of God. Just make sure you obey what God tells *you* to do.

I've found that most Christians are so hooked up to natural thinking that they have made Christianity a sociological experience in fairness. But there is nothing fair about gravity. It works whether or not you believe it. There is nothing "fair" about the laws that govern physics. You just have to find out what are those laws and then act accordingly. But if you try to violate them, you might just become another casualty.

The laws of God work the same way. You can't defy the universal laws that God set in place without unwanted repercussions. Likewise, if you disobey His instructions to you regarding marriage, you will suffer the consequences. So don't try to move God by wailing, "It's not fair! I'm doing more than my spouse is!" Your assignment doesn't change just because your spouse slacks off. God told you in His Word what to do to make your marriage better. Now it's up to you to do it.

⌒ *What's In This For Me?* ⌒

One of the biggest reasons marriages don't work well is *self-centeredness*. People enter marriage with the attitude, "What's in this for me? What can I get out of this relationship? How is my spouse going to meet *my* needs?" They expect their spouse to be their savior, their lover, their friend, their helper, and their biggest cheerleader. They unknowingly place unrealistic expectations on their marriage partner, expecting them to be what only Jesus can be in their lives. It was never God's intention that any human should ever take His place in another person's life.

> ALWAYS REMEMBER IT IS IMPOSSIBLE FOR YOUR PARTNER TO FILL THE PLACE IN *Your Heart* GOD GAVE CHRIST TO FILL.

I've been married long enough to know that marriage is

not the source of joy. Marriage may bring us a lot of good things, including many moments of happiness, but the only thing that can ever bring us joy is *God's presence*. As Psalm 16:11 (KJV) says, *"…in Thy presence is fullness of joy…."*

God didn't give me a marriage so that it would take the place of His presence in my life. If Linda is so wonderful that I let her be *everything* to me, she becomes my idol. God said I am to have no other gods before Him (Exodus 20:3). Jesus must be the central focus of my life. My wife can never be what He is supposed to be to me. And when I take my focus off Him, I risk losing that which He has given me.

None of us should ever lay that heavy burden on our spouse's shoulders. No one but Jesus can fulfill such expectations for us. That's why we always have to look to Him for our fulfillment. Only then can we become tools in His hands to fulfill the dream God has for us as a family unit.

God's Replacement

Many people today seem to think that because they are married, their spouse owes them something. This is a tremendous misconception. I don't owe Linda anything but love. The Bible says we are to owe no man anything except to love him (Romans 13:8). That means everything we do in our marriage is to be based upon our response to our relationship with God — *not* with our spouse.

That's how you make a successful marriage. You come to

understand that your relationship with God is more important to you than your relationship with any other person, including your spouse. Therefore, you do not look to another person to fulfill your needs. You're no longer the little puppy that has to roll over in order to get a treat.

Unfortunately, that's how most couples live their married lives. It's always "If you do this, I'll do this." Everything is based on responding to what the other person does, rather than responding according to their personal relationship with God.

We can never be happy by focusing on the way our spouse needs to be in our marriage. When we start doing that, we slip over into the realm of control and manipulation. We try to make someone else change according to what we want him or her to be. We need to remember that our spouse can never be to us what only Jesus can be. God didn't give our marriage partner to us to replace Him in our lives.

Make your relationship with Jesus the priority of your life. As you do, all other relationships in your life fall in line, especially your marriage relationship. As you seek to honor God and His Word with your life, He shows you how to successfully fulfill your assignment in your marriage relationship.

This principle is so important. For instance, suppose I walk in the house and Linda asks, "Wow, did you have a bad

ACTING ON YOUR Assignment IS A MAJOR KEY TO HAPPINESS.

day, or something?"

I say, "I think I'm doing just fine."

"You're not fine."

"I'm not fine?"

"No, you're not fine."

This discussion can go on all day, and even turn into an argument. Obviously, she says this after picking up something from my facial expression. But no matter what, I cannot afford to respond according to my feelings. In fact, that does us no good at all. My focus should be on what God's Word says about my circumstances. I need to be able to show her chapter and verse for my actions.

Focus On Your Own Assignment

Usually, when married couples get into these kinds of discussions, they spend so much time focusing on what the other spouse doesn't do, that they never do what God called *them* to do. The husband thinks, *"She isn't fulfilling her part in this marriage."* Meanwhile, the wife fumes, *"Why does he get away with everything? Why do I always have to be the one to change?"*

What both must remember is that if one loses, *both lose*. If one doesn't win, *neither wins*. And the only way both can win is if *each focuses on their own assignment*.

This was a principle Peter had to learn after Jesus was

raised from the dead. Peter denied Jesus three times. As the cock crowed, Peter looked up and saw Jesus looking at him with eyes that said, "I wish I hadn't been right about you." After Jesus was crucified, Peter was left to himself in absolute mental and emotional devastation.

A few days later, Peter came out of his hole of despair and decided to go back to his old occupation of fishing with his friends, James and John. (Jesus had been in the grave only a few days, but they had already gone back to their fishing! That doesn't sound like great faith and dedication to me.)

But that morning, Jesus showed up with a fish breakfast (see John 21). He called out to the men in the boat, "Children, have you had any food yet?" Peter couldn't see very well, but John cried out, "It's the Lord!"

Peter got so excited that he put *on* his fisherman's coat and jumped into the water. I haven't figured that one out yet. I mean, instead of just jumping in the water unencumbered, Peter put on his coat (and those fisherman's coats were heavy back then!) and jumped into the water to swim to shore! He must have been too excited to think straight!

Later, as Peter and Jesus sat around the fire eating breakfast, Jesus asked him, "Peter, do you love Me?"

Peter replied, "Lord, You know that I love You."

Jesus said, "Then feed My sheep."

"So let Me ask you another question," Jesus continued. "Do you love Me?"

Peter responded, "Lord, You know I love You."

"Then feed My lambs." In essence, Jesus was saying to Peter, "It is obvious from the way you've been acting that you're not taking care of the spiritual babies. You've only been thinking about your own skin, but you need to take care of My babies."

Then Jesus asked one more time: "Peter, do you love Me?"

Frustrated, Peter quipped, "Lord, You know everything anyway, so what's the difference? Why do You want me to say all this stuff? You know what I've been thinking. You know I went back to fishing after betraying You. You know all the mistakes that I've made. You know how I've been, since You left (*author's paraphrase*)."

Jesus said, "Yes, but I'm going to tell you again, Peter — *feed My sheep*."

At that moment, Peter was reinstated into everything he had lost. It happened that quickly. Then Jesus said to him, "Come on, I need to talk to you about something." Peter was the only one out of all the disciples present who was asked to go on a private walk with Jesus!

Peter had just been forgiven of a huge offense. He had denied Jesus three times at the hour of His greatest need. To be reinstated to a position of favor and responsibility after failing in such a big way must have been a tremendous blessing for Peter. But there was more to come. As Peter and Jesus walked down the beach together, Jesus began to talk to him about his role in feeding the sheep, ruling over the church, and establishing the Kingdom of God in the earth. This was a very strong and extremely important conversation!

Suddenly Peter saw someone out of his peripheral vision. He turned around, and there was John.

Now, John had been somewhat of a "thorn" in Peter's side all along, because he was Jesus' favorite. Knowing this, Peter looked over at John and thought, *"Now is my chance to put John in his place. I'm going to convince Jesus to tell him who I am now."* So Peter asked, "Lord, what about John? What's his role in all this? What will happen to him?"

Everything had been rosy in Jesus' conversation with Peter until that moment. When Peter asked about John, Jesus' posture changed. His countenance changed. He no longer was this nice, calm, raised-from-the-dead Savior. He was now the One whom the book of Revelation calls Faithful and True, sent to judge in righteousness and rule with a rod of iron (*see* Revelation 19)!

With eyes flashing, Jesus firmly responded to Peter, "What is that to you, Peter? What business is that of yours? If I tell you that John will not die until I return, it doesn't have a thing to do with you. You are to do what I told you to do. Don't be wondering what I told him to do. You follow Me and forget about John."

Now, that's exactly what happens in marriage. Marriage partners spend so much time thinking about the failings and shortcomings of their spouse that they never become who *they* are called to be.

The wife says, "If you would love me, I would submit. But you have to go first."

The husband replies, "No, you submit first; then I'll love you!"

The moment we start focusing on the responsibilities of another person instead of on our own responsibilities is the moment we begin to play God in the life of another.

God never expects me to do what He told Linda to do. However, He *has* said that if my wife didn't do what He's told her to do, I am to lead her to the place of reconciliation with Him.

But notice, the issue is *not* whether or not she disobeys *me*; it's whether or not she disobeys *God*. What my wife does in her relationship with me is between her and God, not between her and me. Why? Because I'm called to forgive her, regardless of what she does.

A wife may say to her husband, "I may be disobeying the Word in this marriage, but you still have to show love toward me." Well, now, wait a minute, wives. A disobedient spouse cannot be the one who determines the consequences that come to her life.

Our children often do the same thing after they've been disobedient. They try to negotiate and bargain. Whenever our son Anthony asked for one swat, I'd say three. He'd ask for one swat again, and I'd say four. Needless to say, he quickly gave up that strategy, because the numbers kept getting larger for him!

We often try to do the same thing with God. We attempt to negotiate the consequences for our wrong actions. "Well, this shouldn't happen to me. All I ever did was..." We try to determine the kind of harvest that is produced by our seeds of disobedience to God's Word. But as I am sure you know by now, that is for *God* to determine.

When I act contrary to the Word of God toward my wife, I cannot determine how God wants to correct me for that. "But she didn't treat me right either, and she didn't get in as much trouble as I did!" If I adopt that attitude, I'm going to get in even more trouble. Why? Because God never called me to look at how my wife fulfills her assignment. He called me to look at how I fulfill with *my* assignment as a husband.

To be an excellent marriage partner, you must be a tool of fulfillment in the life of your spouse. You must be a *dream-fulfiller*, not a *dream-killer*. But you can only fill that role in your marriage as you embrace the assignment God gave you.

In 1 Kings 10:8, the queen of Sheba made this comment concerning the men who stood at Solomon's table: *"Happy are your men and happy are these your servants, who stand continually before you and hear your wisdom!"* What was the queen saying? It's very simple. **Our happiness in life is completely dependent upon our willingness to embrace our assignment.**

CHARACTER PRINCIPLES

- Never take authority over something for which Heaven has not made you responsible.

- Respect for another's responsibilities opens the rarely opened door of needed appreciation.

- A healthy home begins with *responsibility* coupled with personal *accountability*, in order to maintain proper balance.

- Always remember: It is impossible for your partner to fill the place in your heart God gave Christ to fill.

- Acting on *your* assignment is a major key to happiness.

CHAPTER 3

Take Out The Trash

One of the most common reasons couples have a difficult time in their marriages is that one or both of them didn't come to the relationship as a whole person. Many come into the marriage with some type of dysfunctional "baggage" from the past, which adversely affects their present behavior. But a healthy marriage requires both husband and wife to be whole, transparent, and non-threatening.

Couples often think they should postpone getting married until they attain a measure of success on the outside of their lives — for instance, until they make enough money to live well together. But the better reason to wait is this: They need to know they're ready for marriage *on the inside*. That means getting rid of childhood baggage *before* taking their marriage vows!

CONTRARY TO POPULAR OPINION, PAST EXPERIENCES DO NOT HAVE TO DETERMINE PRESENT Attitudes.

If the person you are thinking about marrying has problems now, be cautious. Everything is NOT going to get better just because you get married! Unless you both go into the marriage determined to become everything God called you to be, those problems will only multiply back to you. They will feel like a chain around your neck that gets tighter and tighter, choking all the life and the joy out of you.

Recognize Your Past

Husbands, if your character was lacking when you entered into your marriage, don't expect your wife to cover or offset those weaknesses. Wives, if you were deeply hurt by a previous relationship, don't expect your husband to heal those wounds or atone for another's cruelty. Only Jesus can make you the whole person you need to be in order to make your marriage work! Your marriage can never flourish as long as you hide behind your dysfunctional "fig-leaf apron" and make your spouse try to figure out what is bothering you.

"Yes, but you don't know what people did to me in the past."

I may not know the details of your past, but I do know what it's like to have people take advantage of you. I know what it's like to have others' negative words cut and tear at your soul.

Though situations may have occurred in your past, do you think it's fair or right to allow someone who isn't even in your marriage to speak louder to you than the one who is married to you?

I remember the day someone asked me, "Who has been the most influential person in your life?" Of course we each have a different answer to that question, but many people immediately think of their most *positive* influence, such as, "My mom. She has always been such a wonderful example." Or someone else might answer, "My grandfather. He taught me so much."

But after pondering the question, I replied, "The person who has had the most influence on any of our lives is the person who has caused us the most pain." I was correct. In other words, the person who influences our lives the most is the one who causes us to *no longer trust*. Because of that individual's influence, we begin to isolate ourselves from people and close the door to transparent intimacy.

ᐧ Find The True Offender ᐧ

Too often, the wife is blamed for something in her husband's past with which she had nothing to do. Conversely, the husband is blamed for what other men did to his wife before they were married.

When you live in the hurts of the past, you end up making your spouse pay for what someone else did to you. You blame the one you are with, instead of the one who actually wronged you. If you are ever going to be whole, you need to recognize the true offender. Then you need to forgive that person and let that be the end of it.

Some women get married just because they want to get out of the house in which they grew up. However, although they are physically out of the house, the house is still inside of them!

That was the problem God faced with the children of Israel. He could get the Israelites out of Egypt; He just couldn't get Egypt out of the Israelites!

So make the decision never to let an influence from your past determine the nature of your present marriage relationship. No matter from where you came, refuse to bring the negative leftovers from your yesterdays into the home you are establishing today.

Committed

PARTNERS CHOOSE
TO TURN THEIR
WRONG DECISIONS
INTO RIGHT
CONCLUSIONS.

But what if you're dealing with your spouse's "negative leftovers"? What if you're married, and you secretly wish you weren't? Well, you have a choice. You can stand all day in front of the mirror, pointing a finger at yourself, saying, "Shame on you for marrying the person you married!" *Or* you can do it God's way and start believing in the person you chose as your spouse.

Our Negative Leftovers

Linda chose to marry me when I was a drug addict and a drunk, going nowhere. Quite frankly she shouldn't have married me. She either had a mental lapse — or she was the most brilliant woman on her block (I prefer to think that she was brilliant!).

Meanwhile, I married Linda because she was the happiest person I had ever met in my life. I figured if I could just keep that happy person around me all the time, she would make me happy. I thought that was how marriage worked, but I was wrong. So we both made wrong choices — we got married for the wrong reasons. And to be honest, neither one of us thought we would stay married for more than a year and a half.

But about the time Linda and I had predicted we'd break up, I got born again — and that changed everything! God taught us how to turn our wrong decisions into right conclusions, *by choice*.

I'm a living testimony that a man *can* change. Linda and I weren't born again when we first got married, and, to put it bluntly, I was a real jerk — a rat to the tenth power. I'm telling you, I was a bad rat! I used to tell her, "You better keep it straight in our relationship, Sweetheart, because if you don't, you can just put your clothes in the suitcase and head on out. It doesn't matter to me — someone else will be waiting in line to take your place by morning!"

I did everything I could to make that girl reject me. However, in spite of it all, Linda loved me. She kissed the ground I walked on! She was out-of-this-world wonderful to me!

Before we got married, Linda used to come to my house at six o'clock every morning to make breakfast for me. She didn't have a car at that time, but every day she rode her bike three and a half miles to where I worked to bring me a hot lunch. I decided, *"I may have been born at night, but I wasn't born LAST night! I need to marry this woman so she doesn't get away!"*

We had been married about a year and a half when I got born again. Suddenly I entered into an entirely new love for Linda that I couldn't explain. God put such a deep love for her in my heart, that I would have done anything for her. I was head over heels in love with that lady, and I started showing my love to her in every way I could possibly think of. (To this very day, I don't know a man who treats his wife better than I treat Linda.)

Linda got born again about a month after I did, and everything was absolutely wonderful for about a year. Then I began to notice that the woman who had always been so loving, forgiving, and understanding toward me suddenly acquired a "wicked witch of the west" broom, and she knew how to use it!

That wasn't supposed to happen! We had just become Christians, so our marriage was supposed to be getting better, not worse!

Finally, I couldn't take it anymore. I said to Linda, "Honey, please help me here. I need to ask you a question. While I was a stupid, mean jerk who treated you terribly, you loved me. You tolerated my behavior. You made me believe there couldn't possibly be another woman in the world as resilient as you. I kept trying to get rid of you, and you kept bouncing back. You did everything for me that I could have possibly desired. Now I've changed. I can't imagine not having you in my life. I'm doing all I can to love you and take care of you. But all of a sudden, it seems like someone else has come to live in your body! What in the world happened to you? Why are you suddenly so rebellious?"

Linda's reply was profound to me. She said, *Because now I know that you will never leave me.*

What did my wife mean by that? Linda had been motivated to treat me well when we first met because she was afraid that I would reject her and leave her. (The root of that fear went all the way back to her childhood; I had just never recognized it before.) But once she was convinced I had truly changed, she started feeling safe enough to expose those fears and hurts.

During that difficult period, there were times I wasn't sure our marriage was going to make it. But, thank God, we finally got off that rocky road and started traveling the road to recovery.

Forgive Yourself

For years Linda and I had to work on erasing her fear of rejection, and it wasn't always easy. The road to recovery was riddled with pain, but at each stage of our growth, we chose to walk in forgiveness and to focus on the next level of building our marriage!

Don't waste your time blaming yourself for yesterday. It doesn't do any good to try to make yesterday better. You cannot. Just make sure you don't repeat the same mistake tomorrow. We all make mistakes, but we don't have to keep on making the same mistakes over and over again.

And let me say this before I go any further: Stop looking for a perfect person to marry. I know a number of people who believed they married the perfect person, only to find out later that their "perfect person" wasn't perfect after all.

Wives, perhaps you have regrets about the man you chose to marry, because you found out since then that he isn't what you thought him to be. "But I thought he was the right one for me! How could I have missed it?" you may have thought in despair. Well, your husband may very well be the *right* one, but that doesn't mean he is the *perfect* one, because the perfect person doesn't exist.

Here's another consideration: It is important to know that men and women deal very differently with conflict. When boys disagree over an issue, they knock each other down and make each other bleed; but then they get back up and are friends again.

EACH TIME WE ACCUSE ANOTHER, WE ARE MOST OFTEN GUILTY OF THE SAME *Trespass* OURSELVES.

But girls are different. They talk about each other. They hold grudges longer than boys. They let issues bother them for long periods of time — even if they have actually forgotten what the grudge is all about!

Years ago I watched Linda struggle with this problem. Linda's dad spent more than forty years on the road as a truck driver. During much of her childhood, he was only home one day each week, and sometimes less. Now, I understand that Linda's dad worked hard because of his love for his wife and children. He worked to take care of his family and to do what was right. However, he will never know what I have had to deal with because of his absenteeism. He will never know how strongly Linda has attempted to hold on to certain things in our marriage because he was home so little as she grew up. Linda has had to learn how to let go of that hurt.

That's something we all have to do in order to build an excellent marriage. In John 20:23, Jesus explained why: *"If you forgive the sins of any, they are forgiven them; if you retain the sins of any, they are retained."*

Jesus said in part that whatever consequences from past hurts are brought into your new life, those consequences don't affect the person who sinned against you; *they affect you.* Unless you forgive that person and let go of the offense, the consequences are now upon *you* — they affect your present relationships, especially your marriage.

That's why it's so important to avoid passing judgment on people, including your spouse. Also, make sure that you never use God's Word to your advantage against your spouse. Only use the Word to edify and to help set him or her free.

It never bothers me when Linda brings me a scripture from an accurate perspective; I don't have a problem with that. But I do have a problem when a person takes a scripture out of context and makes it what he wants it to be, in order to control and manipulate a situation or to justify his fleshly behavior. God's Word is a weapon to be used against the devil, not against our spouse. Only when you accurately and appropriately use God's Word can you take the position in your marriage that God called you to fill.

Cultivating A "No-Fault" Marriage

What do I mean when I say that you and your spouse need to learn to live in a "no-fault" relationship? Although it may be technically true that someone is the cause of a certain set of unwanted circumstances, you and your spouse must never indulge in the temptation to blame each other. Don't allow yourselves to play the blame game; just fix the problem. When you blame your spouse to win a dispute, your don't win anything — *you actually both lose.* Your marriage relationship loses, because you destroy transparency and create alienation. Since

> THE BLAME GAME IS A POOR SUBSTITUTE FOR LIVING IN A NO-FAULT *Relationship* WITH SOMEONE YOU SAY YOU LOVE.

you're going to be married for the rest of your lives, why not enjoy your time together, instead of wasting your days pointing your fingers at each other?

Here's another way to look at it. Husbands, the Bible tells you that when you love your wife, you love yourself (Ephesians 5:28). Do you blame yourself for everything that goes wrong? The truth is, you'd actually be better off going into the bathroom and pointing your finger at the guy in the mirror, than to point that finger at your wife. Verse 29 says that no man hates his own flesh. Yet every time you treat your wife in a negative way, that's the way you treat yourself; you hate your own flesh.

Remember, she is the part of you that you don't understand. The very qualities she possesses happen to be the qualities God took out of you. She isn't strange; she is just different than you are. And God gave her to you to add value to your life.

Understand something: Hatred stirs up strife, but love covers all sins (Proverbs 15:18, 1 Peter 4:8). While hatred is at the core of blaming, love is at the core of covering. That's why there is never to be any faultfinding in a marriage relationship. As 2 Corinthians 5:16 says, we are not to see others "according to the flesh," or from a worldly point of view.

If you and your spouse are both born again, one of the greatest revelations you'll ever have about your marriage is that both of you are also the righteousness of God in Christ. That means you can't treat yourself as a new creature in Christ and, at the same time, treat your spouse as an old creature.

Soon after I accepted Christ, I understood that if my old self had been crucified with Him, Linda's old self had been crucified with Christ as well (Romans 6:6). If I was the righteousness of God in Christ, so was she (2 Corinthians 5:21). So I couldn't walk around with an attitude that said I was okay but there was something wrong with her. No, I had to learn to see both my wife *and* myself according to God's Word.

Therefore, in my marriage, Linda is never at fault. My love for her covers everything, faults and all. After all, why would I want to blame and find fault with the one I love, nourish, and cherish? She is a treasure. She is the righteousness of God in Christ. She adds value to my life. Therefore, I'm not interested in pointing a finger in her direction. I just want to focus on what I need to do to be a better husband to her.

Besides, whenever I'm tempted to get into strife with

Linda, I just remember that God is her Protector. As His daughter, God takes care of her. So I make sure that I never step over the boundaries that God set for me in our marriage relationship. I am thus able to focus on resolving any conflict according to His Word.

I know that correctly resolving marital conflict can be a difficult thing to do, but you simply must learn how to do it, if you're ever going to have a lasting and fulfilling marriage. The most essential key I've found to resolve conflict God's way is this: *Although it is important to know who you are, it is even more important to know who you are NOT.*

In other words, you must first be willing to accept the position God gave you in your marriage; then you must recognize and respect the position your spouse holds.

Careless Speech

Let's take this a little further. In Ephesians 4:29, God commands, *"Let no corrupt word proceed out of your mouth, but what is good for necessary edification, that it may impart grace to the hearers."* Now, when God says no corrupt word, that's exactly what He means!

In the context of marriage, God says you are to allow *no unkind, unnecessary, foul, or putrid words* to proceed out of your mouth in your marriage relationship. In other words, every word that comes out of your mouth is to build up, encourage, and add value to your spouse. That is how you fulfill verse 30: "*And do not grieve the Holy Spirit of God…*"

That word "grieve" refers to a very deep hurt. God says that whenever you speak unkind words to the one He places in your life, you do not just hurt your spouse; you hurt the Holy Spirit. You are treating the righteousness of God with unkindness, and that deeply grieves the Spirit of God.

ASTUTE PARTNERS ARE ACUTELY AWARE OF THIS FACT: THEY ARE *Accountable* FOR EVERY WORD THEY SPEAK.

I know so many married couples today that might say wonderful things about their mates to other people, but when they are with their spouse, they tear them down and constantly engage in hurtful dialogue. My advice to these couples is this: Don't be so interested in what you say to other people about your spouse. Be more interested in what you say *to your spouse*. Remember, "*Death and life are in the power of the tongue…*" (Proverbs 18:21).

Ephesians 4:31-32 goes on to give sound advice that married couples should heed:

> Let all bitterness, wrath, anger, clamor, and evil speaking be put away from you, with all malice. And be kind to one another, tenderhearted, forgiving one another, just as God in Christ forgave you.

Just imagine — God spoke these words to the most spiritual, mature church in all of the New Testament Scriptures! He also says these words to us, as husbands and wives: "Stop being mean to each other. Get rid of the bitter, sarcastic tone of voice. Stop speaking behind one another's back in a negative way. Don't use demeaning words that cut and hurt each other. Rather, use words that are positive and encouraging. Above all, be kind and forgiving to each other, just as I am with you."

⇒ Put Your Trust In God ⇒

As I mentioned earlier, if one or both partners brings emotional "baggage" into the marriage, *trust* becomes an issue. How can you separate love and trust in a marriage relationship? It's very simple. You're called to trust God with everything. But if you trust in fellow frail human beings, you're going to be tremendously disappointed.

Think about it. How many times have you been disappointed by another person? Probably more times than you care to count. But have you ever been disappointed by God? No, because God *can't* lie. Never once has He been unfaithful to His Word. Now, you may have thought that

> YOU ARE CALLED TO *Trust God* AND LOVE YOUR SPOUSE, NOT LOVE GOD, AND TRUST YOUR SPOUSE.

God disappointed you at one time or another in your life. But the truth is, when you fulfill *your part* in obedience to the Word, you never have occasion to feel like God disappoints you. *God's promises always come to pass for the obedient.* That's why you are never to put your trust in a person; you are to trust only in God.

A husband might say, "My wife cheated on me. I don't think I can ever trust her again." To that husband, I say, "Trusting her was your first mistake." You must *trust* your marriage relationship to God and *love* your marriage partner. That is the only way to live beyond the fear and paranoia of betrayal.

Think about it — worrying about what your spouse may do wrong isn't going to stop him or her from doing it. So why in the world do you waste your time worrying about it? Worrying just makes you fall apart internally, while your offending spouse — the one who's causing the pain — moves along unscathed.

You have to roll your cares about your spouse onto the Lord. Stop worrying about the situation, whatever it is. If your spouse makes the right choices and comes through the situation a stronger Christian, praise the Lord for it. But if he or she *doesn't* come through victoriously, keep praising the Lord anyway. God will protect you and bless you in spite of a disobedient spouse, as you stay obedient to His Word.

So keep trusting God and loving your spouse, regardless of

the challenges you face. We must never put our trust in human beings, or the day will come when we say, "I love You, Lord, but why did You let this happen to me?" The answer will be obvious: "Because you trusted in a mere human." You must put your trust in the Lord and then focus on loving your spouse.

Let me recap some of the valuable lessons we've discussed so far.

1. Recognize your respective positions in your marriage relationship.
2. Dump the baggage from the past.
3. Stay personally accountable to the Word of God for your actions, words, and attitudes toward your marriage partner.
4. What you do or say is never your spouse's problem. He or she isn't at fault for anything wrong that is going on inside your home; nor are you ever at fault for what your spouse does or says.

The fact is that none of us know the Word of God in entirety. We only know a little in any area of life; and wherever we lack the knowledge of God's Word, we fail miserably.

So stop trying to blame your spouse for your problems, and just admit that you also have faults. Remember, you are not what you think you are; you are what you do. Matthew 12:34 says, "...*out of the abundance of the heart the mouth speaks.*"

Begin to find out who you are by watching your trail.

Don't ever trust yourself to the point that you think you "have it together," or that you don't need to work on your life. Listen to your words and observe your actions, to find out what you *really* believe. Then if you find an area in which you don't measure up to God's Word, do something about it.

Don't feel discouraged when challenged in some area of your life. Just recognize it as an indication to you that it's time to go back to the drawing board and make some adjustments. Allow God's Word to work in your heart and change you from the inside out.

That's the first step — be willing to *change*. Make a life-long commitment to take the position God gave you and to become everything He called you to be in your marriage. Refuse to abandon that assigned position, even for a moment. As both you and your spouse take these steps toward building a lasting, successful marriage, the day will come when you will hear God say, "The two have truly become one flesh!"

CHAPTER PRINCIPLES

- Contrary to popular opinion, past experiences do not have to determine present attitudes.

- Committed partners *choose* to turn their wrong decisions into right conclusions.

- Each time we accuse another, we are most often guilty of the same trespass ourselves.

- The "blame-game" is a poor substitute for living in a no-fault relationship with someone you say you love.

- Astute partners are acutely aware of this fact: They are accountable for every word they speak.

- You are called to trust God and love your spouse, not love God and trust your spouse.

CHAPTER 4

What Makes Them Tick

I believe God has provided for us vital keys to unlock the mysteries of an excellent marriage. He has made these keys available to anyone who cares enough to seek them out in His Word and use them.

We're going to look at several of these keys that, when followed, will help you and your spouse achieve the fulfilling marriage for which you long. As you read these principles, keep in mind that they don't just apply to marriage, but also to your relationships in every arena of life — friends, co-workers, church family, etc. That's important to understand, because you can't successfully develop excellence in one area and ignore the other areas of your life. Otherwise, the excellence you achieve in the one area will only spotlight the areas you are neglecting, leaving you unfulfilled.

⌁ *A Healthy Foundation* ⌁

Before we get into these principles, know this: *An excellent marriage has to be built on an excellent foundation.* The building process begins with finding the scriptural purpose for entering into marriage in the first place.

Why do two people get married? Ultimately, they get married to solve a problem for each other, although they often misinterpret exactly which problem that is.

What do I mean by that? Most people enter into marriage for *themselves.* They want to be taken care of. They long to be happy. They crave to satisfy their physical desires. They don't want to be alone. They yearn to settle down and raise a family.

But getting married for any of these reasons is a recipe for disappointment and heartache. Believers are never to enter any relationship — *especially* marriage — for self-centered reasons. Our motive should always be to give something rather than to *get* something.

> THE RIGHT MARRIAGE PARTNERS KNOW WHEN THEY ENTERED MARRIAGE THEY DID IT FOR *Their Spouse* NOT FOR THEMSELVES.

Let's look at a common assumption held by many people: *Marriage will make me happier.* Paul says in 1 Corinthians 7:40 that people would actually be happier if they remained *un*married! Was Paul speaking against marriage? No, he was saying, "I know that those who get married will have trouble in the flesh" (*see* v. 28).

It is a fact that a happy marriage brings tremendous blessings into your lives, and, personally, I wouldn't have it any other way. But we have to accept the fact that there are trials that go along with marriage. Paul tells us why in verses 32-34:

> In everything you do, I want you to be free from the concerns of this life. An unmarried man can spend his time doing the Lord's work and thinking how to please Him. But a married man can't do that so well. He has to think about his earthly responsibilities and how to please his wife. His interests are divided.
>
> In the same way, a woman who is no longer married or has never been married can be more devoted to the Lord in body and in spirit, while the married woman must be concerned about her earthly responsibilities and how to please her husband.
>
> 1 Corinthians 7:32-34 (NLT)

Prior to marriage, a man's life is largely uncomplicated. He doesn't have to give much thought to anything other than God, work, his car, and which TV dinner to cook on a given night! But after he says those wedding vows, he has to start thinking about what is going on in his wife's life. He has someone else to please, besides the Lord.

Sometimes a husband wants to bring the independence of his single lifestyle into his marriage. He doesn't think he needs to answer his wife's questions. He feels he doesn't need to tell her where he's going or how long he'll be gone.

Let me tell you something, husbands. It gives your wife security to know where you are. When she doesn't know, the enemy comes to your house and starts talking to her. Soon jealousy sets in and trust begins to erode. She starts to feel overprotective, and you start to feel smothered. That isn't the way God intends marriage to be. A husband can give his wife great security by staying considerate of her needs.

The truth is that after you get married, you have nothing left that belongs only to you. You don't have your own space or time, and neither does your wife. You both made the choice to become one. Hence, one of the biggest priorities of your lives should be to learn how to please each other.

Your responsibility to please the one you married isn't a negative thing at all. It doesn't mean you have no more time to pursue spiritual matters. God is still to have first place in your life. You're still to seek Him continually, "Lord, what is it that You have for my life? I want to do everything You want me to do." But here is a wonderful thought: Now you have a new way of pleasing the Lord — *by seeking to please your spouse!*

Sure, life would be a lot easier if all I had to do was get out of bed every morning, fall on my knees, and pray all day. But that isn't everything I need to do. I need to consider what is going on with Linda. What time is she going to be home? What is her emotional state today? Is she thinking that I'm not spending enough time at home lately? Is she happy with our marriage?

∾ Please One Another ∾

These types of thoughts constantly run through a Godly husband's mind. Of course, not all husbands pay attention to them. But the Bible says, "...*a married man is concerned about the affairs of this world — how he can please his wife*" (v. 33, NIV). The husband is to find ways to please his wife so there may be harmony in the home.

So how do you lay the bedrock of an excellent foundation for your marriage? You don't go into marriage for yourself; you go into marriage for your spouse. You don't enter the marriage covenant so you can acquire a big ring for your finger or so you can say, "I'm married to that person." You go into marriage because you believe you're the best person in the world for your spouse and that your spouse is the best person in the world for you.

Husbands, before you get married, it's important to ask yourself, "Am I the best person for this woman? Do I love her enough? Am I committed enough to want the best for her?" If not, you should be willing to back out of the relationship, because you want the best for *her*, not just for *yourself*.

Throughout your life together, both of you should maintain this selfless attitude toward each other, for an excellent marriage can be built on no other foundation.

Wives, ask the Lord, "Father, how can I please my husband? How can I be everything he wants me to be, and help him become all You have called *him* to be?" Pleasing your husband, *not yourself*, should become your primary focus, for in pleasing him, you please the Lord.

So many married couples miss it right here in this area. They get married for what they can *get* rather than for what they can *give*. As a result, almost six out of ten marriages in the United States end in divorce. Although that's a horrible statistic, I'll tell you what bothers me even more — the church isn't very far behind! In fact, some studies put us a bit beyond that.

Fifty percent of all Christian marriages end in divorce, and this is the main reason for this sorry situation: Believers enter marriage for the wrong reasons. As they build their relationships on faulty, self-centered foundations, their problems multiply and their marriages eventually crumble.

Here's the dilemma I see again and again: When a man marries a woman, he wants her to stay exactly the way she was when he met her. On the other hand, when a woman finds a husband, she genuinely believes she can change him into what she wants him to be. When she says, "I do," she often thinks, "Well, it's time to get to work on this man!" The problem is, the opposite usually happens in both cases: Men generally stay the same, and women almost always change!

If a man was an ugly slob before he got married, he probably still will be an ugly slob ten years after he gets married. Meanwhile, she may change from someone who loves to serve his every need to someone who acts like the wicked witch of the west!

So let me give a word of warning to you if you are still single: *Never marry anyone who isn't already whole.* If you make that mistake, you will begin your marriage by jumping into a hole that you will spend most of your life digging out of. You will find yourself in the position of continually propping up your spouse, as you try to help him or her become a whole person.

Remember, you can only prop up people for so long before you have to let them settle wherever they're going to settle. After a while, you just have to let them deal with their own problems and the condition of their own soul. That can be very difficult to do with a spouse, because in so many ways, their problems directly affect you!

Some women say, "But I just need a man in my life!" This is a deception. What they *really* need is acceptance. They want to know that they are loved — that they are chosen. That's why it's so important for a woman to understand how much God loves her. If she knows that, she won't go looking out of God's will for some man to love her.

The same principle is true for men. A wise man might be lured to a gorgeous girl, for her looks. This kind of woman seems wonderful until she says something; then it often becomes obvious that he put more confidence in her *looks* than in her *character*. As the Bible says, charm is deceitful, and beauty is fleeting (Proverbs 31:30). Charm and beauty are not the qualities on which to base a decision that lasts for a lifetime!

So we see that an excellent marriage starts with a scriptural purpose, as both partners enter into the covenant. Both must have a heart to give of themselves to the other.

ᴄ Get Ready For Change ᴄ

The next requirement for a happy marriage is simple: *Each must be willing to change*.

"I can't believe he wants me to do that! I'm *not* going to change just because he wants me to change!" That's an example of a rebellious attitude — a deadly poison in a marriage relationship. A spouse who is unwilling to change for the benefit of his or her spouse is in a state of rebellion.

DEVOTED MARRIAGE PARTNERS MAINTAIN A CONSISTENT *Willingness* TO CHANGE FOR THE BENEFIT OF THEIR SPOUSE.

Whenever I come to realize I need to make an adjustment that will be to the benefit of someone else, I change right away. It doesn't matter to me if it's inconvenient or difficult for me to change. I do it anyway, because to refuse is to be rebellious toward God or His Word.

"Oh, but that's just the way I am," some say. That's the kind of attitude that has made so many married couples miserable for so long. Sadly, it's not uncommon to find seventy-five or eighty-year-old couples who have despised each other for decades!

They might say, "Yes, but at least we've stayed together all these years."

I tell them, "Are you kidding? You haven't been *together* for the last forty years! 'Together' *doesn't* mean you survived from killing each other! It means you have your home in divine order. It means you do what the Word says."

That kind of marriage is a mockery of the Gospel. The Gospel brings *victory* into a person's life. It doesn't put people in a defensive holding position. It's not about holding on as long as you can, and merely enduring everything the enemy throws at your marriage.

An unwillingness to change is at the root of mediocrity in marriage. And a person's mediocre attitude about his responsibilities in the marriage is at the heart of spousal withdrawal.

For instance, a mediocre wife may say, "Well, at least I'm a good cook." Yes, but if it's good food that he wants, he can always find that at a good restaurant.

A man draws away from the woman he married if she has a poor attitude about her role as his wife. The same thing happens when a husband has a mediocre attitude. Eventually the wife will draw away from him, feeling rejected.

People say that most marriages end in divorce court because of money problems. But I believe the issue is attitude.

When a marriage partner has a poor attitude, the other spouse feels controlled and trapped. But if, instead, that partner consistently loves, forgives, embraces, and commits to building a great marriage, it is impossible for the other spouse to walk away!

I've done a lot of things right in my marriage, but there have been some things about which I haven't been so right. As a matter of fact, as each day passes, I discover more and more things I'm really not very good at.

But one thing is for sure — I don't say words I don't mean. Couples often "blow sunshine" at each other, giving out cheap compliments they don't even mean. They think if they just blow enough sunshine, they can cause the clouds to go away. How untrue that is!

Believe The Best Of Each Other

Whenever a storm looms on the horizon in my home, Linda and I are quick to boldly declare, "We will *not* have any invaders to our home. Nothing will mess up the harmony we enjoy in this place!" In doing so, we are able to diffuse problems before they birth calamity for our family.

I'll give you an example. After a long day at the office dealing with others' demands and problems, or after having words with someone, I am ready for the peaceful atmosphere of home. However, I may walk in the door and see some

things that are out of order — and my close
associates will tell you that I have a
great passion for order. I might immediately want to know why things are
not in order in our home.

LEARN
THE ART OF
Diffusing
POTENTIAL PROBLEMS
BEFORE THEY
START.

Did you ever get into an argument
with your spouse or children that really
had nothing to do with them? I have. Many
times those who are closest to us catch the shrapnel from a
"bomb" that was fired at us through someone else. Sadly, our
family often has nothing to do with it!

My demand to know why I've come home to a disorderly
house has all the makings of a potential storm or argument.
But Linda in her wisdom quickly diffuses the problem by asking soothingly, "What can I do for you, Robb? What can I get
for you? We can talk later about it. Let's just relax for a little
while. Everything will be fine."

Responding with love and wisdom is something both you
and your spouse can do for each other. When you see a storm
brewing on the horizon, become willing to be whatever the
other person needs at that moment. In this way, you submit
yourselves one to another in the fear of God (Ephesians 5:21).

God doesn't want you to further agitate and antagonize
your spouse, even when he or she is having a "flesh-flash" or
self-control challenges. That is never God's way of doing
things. To become an understanding marriage partner, learn

how to diffuse potential problems before they really begin. If you and your spouse are willing to do that, you will never need to have another fight!

Decide To Have A Good Attitude

In Romans 12:21, God tells us not to respond to evil with evil, but to overcome evil with good. If marriage partners commit to continually overcoming evil with good in their relationships, eventually evil will subside completely.

If I come home with a wrong attitude, Linda has a choice. She can respond with the same type of attitude, which will inevitably lead to conflict, or she can overcome my bad attitude by changing the atmosphere.

An *Understanding* MARRIAGE PARTNER NEVER RESPONDS TO AN ATTITUDE WITH AN ATTITUDE.

The truth is that life is wound up so tight these days that a good attitude is a rarity. Many times we hold our mates to standards to which we ourselves would never want to be held. So when our spouse fails to meet our expectations, we react with a poor attitude, and everything goes downhill from there!

I understand that the natural tendency is to react in kind when someone comes to you with a poor attitude. But that only makes the situation worse.

Linda has had to deal with me after talking to lawyers and bankers, to spiritual babies who don't want to grow, and to self-centered Christians who always want their way. At times like that, I feel all wound up and a little self-centered myself, because I've given out so much. But thank God for the gift of an understanding spouse who knows how to diffuse these emotional fallouts.

If you and your spouse don't understand how to embrace one another when you've given out so much in the other areas of your life, you're going to endure constant conflict. You're going to start thinking, *"My spouse is my problem."*

Now, remember, I deal with a lot of church and ministry matters that Linda doesn't know about. She and I talk all the time, but there are things that she doesn't know — people I talk to around the world, things that are said to me, tasks I need to perform, and so forth. My life is very detailed, but my communication is not. Too often I just assume that Linda understands what I mean without any explanation on my part.

I guess I think I'm a computer, and my wife just needs to plug in to me to get the information! The opposite is actually true. Quite often, it is I who needs to download information to her.

There has been a time or two through the years that Linda knew, as soon as I walked into the house, that I didn't walk in alone — I brought an unwelcome spirit with me. I inadvertently carried a destroyer home with me. So she opens her arms to *me*, while at the same time denying access to that spirit; but there have been a few times when she has responded to my poor attitude with her own poor attitude, irritably asking me, "Robb, what is wrong with you?"

"Nothing is wrong with me. What's wrong with *you*?"

"I'm fine. You're the one with an attitude."

"Who do you think you are, talking to me like that? I understand what the Bible has to say about attitudes, but I'm not sure *you* do."

"Why is it you can always find the part of the Bible that supports your point of view, but never mine?"

Hurtful words fly as we get into heated exchanges. An argument like this could go on for days at a time — but it could be avoided if spouses learned to respond to the other's poor attitude with a good one.

That's why Romans 12:21 says that we are not to respond to evil with evil. Instead, we are to overcome evil with good.

Strife: The Marriage Killer!

Understand this: The number-one destroyer of marriages is *strife*. This toxic enemy gets into a home through unresolved disagreements. One or both spouses hold tight to their own opinions, thinking they know better than the other.

In fact, most marriages don't break up because the husband and wife don't love each other anymore (even though that is what they may say). Marriages usually break up because the husband and wife don't *like* each other anymore. The qualities that attracted them to each other in the first place are no longer there.

Newlyweds often get disheartened when they get hit by a sudden onslaught of conflict after wedlock. They forget that the deeper the commitment between two people, the more opportunity there is for disagreement.

People who are not committed to each other really don't care if they disagree about things. But when you put your trust in someone, you begin to be interested in what they say and how they treat others. Why? Because if they take advantage of others, they will ultimately take advantage of you. Thus, you are more watchful of what they say and do because of your commitment to them.

Remember when you were dating the person you married? You didn't tolerate hours of broken fellowship between the two of you. If you had a disagreement, you did everything you could possibly do to quickly settle it and reconcile. You worked at your relationship. You were excited to marry this person who was so easy to make up with.

But after the wedding, something often happens. *You stop making up after arguments.* You begin to put more energy into arguments and less energy into forgiveness and reconciliation. Stand-offs, with cold wars lasting days, become more and more frequent. Finally, the two of you realize that you don't even like being with each other anymore. Before you know it, you are talking about divorce.

How do you keep from scheduling that kind of destruction for your own marriage? By not letting yourselves live in one *moment* of discord in your home. Walk in love with each other. Life is too short and too precious for you to waste it in disharmony and strife!

Before you ever get into another argument, make a quality decision together that you will make up with as much intensity (or even greater) as you fight one another. Set down that decision in concrete, before the difficulties come. Your relationship will always stay healthy as you both run toward reconciliation with a greater fervor than you run toward a fight!

After you both make that decision, you'll find that disagreements between the two of you become much less frequent. It will not be uncommon to stop right in the middle of your argument, smile at each other, and say, "I can hardly wait to make up!"

Commit To Resolve

When you hit a relational impasse with your spouse, do you stop and set up camp, or do you make a commitment to resolve it and move on? Many times, what starts as a small misunderstanding between spouses soon becomes a stubborn standoff that lasts for hours or even days. Since neither party is willing to repent, the problem just gets shelved until the next irritant arises.

Has your marriage turned into a perpetual domestic "tug-of-war," with invisible lines drawn down the center of the home — the husband pulling one way, and the wife the other way?

Here is what you can do. In the name of Jesus, take authority over the strife that has overtaken your home. Ask God to forgive you both for participating in hurtful, selfish behavior, and then commit to resolve.

Then when strife reappears (and it will), be quick to repent for your part in it. That's one thing I really appreciate about Linda. She doesn't lose any time before repenting. She was the firstborn in her family and has a firstborn's "quick-to-spout-off" nature. But she is also quick to admit her fault and get in the penalty box for "high-lipping"!

If you want an excellent marriage, learn how to develop a "you-win" attitude. Respond to every situation with the attitude, "What does *my spouse* get out of this situation?" rather than "What do *I* get of it?" Don't expect to always have a "win-win" outcome to every situation.

The Bible says in Proverbs 15:1, "*A soft answer turns away wrath...*" As you learn to respond with a soft answer and a good attitude, you will stop the ever-escalating cycle of strife before it ever starts.

We need to always keep in mind that the way we treat the people around us is the way we treat God. In Matthew 10:40, Jesus said, "*He who receives you receives Me, and he who receives Me receives Him who sent Me."*

Many Christians don't understand this connection between their relationship with their spouse and their relationship with God. They can come out of a time of deep intercession or fasting and be the meanest dog to their spouse!

⌐ *Self-Acceptance* ⌐

Unless I receive Linda the way I receive Jesus, I don't have Linda and I don't have Jesus. If I don't receive her, I don't receive the One who sent Jesus. But if I do receive her as a gift from God, then Jesus comes with her. I don't have to jockey for position with her; I just have to love her and receive her. As I do this, Jesus comes and lives within our marriage.

THE WAY YOU *Treat Your Spouse* IS THE WAY YOU BELIEVE GOD TREATS YOU.

The problem in many of our marriages is that we make our spouse continually re-qualify for access and acceptance every day. How many more times do we need to be told we are loved, before we finally believe it? If we don't believe a person can love us, we certainly don't believe God loves us!

We may say, "Yes, but my wife doesn't really seem to respect me" or "My husband doesn't pay enough attention to me. He never tells me that he loves me." Well, that doesn't matter, because *God* says, in Psalm 139:14, that we are fearfully and wonderfully made. Once we grab on to that truth, we don't need anyone else to prop us up or stroke our ego.

If a wife doesn't believe she is fearfully and wonderfully made, her husband could tell her that he loves her every three minutes, twenty-four hours a day, seven days a week, and she still wouldn't hear it. She'd still say, "You never tell me that you love me," because the voice inside her always speaks louder than any voice on the outside. The problem isn't that her husband doesn't love her. It's that she doesn't love herself.

The same can be said about whether or not a husband believes his wife respects him. She can demonstrate her respect towards him in a countless number of ways, but if he does not respect or believe in himself, he will never be convinced of her esteem, honor, and deep regard.

That's why the Bible says we shall have whatsoever we say (Mark 11:23). That's why it says a man is whatever he thinks in *his* heart (Proverbs 23:7). It isn't what other people say that determines the outcome of our lives; it is what we say to *ourselves*.

I will never make my wife re-qualify for me. If I did that, I would only have a relationship with her that was one day deep and 10,000 days long! Instead, our marriage relationship is 10,000 days deep and gets deeper as each day passes.

Linda knows, beyond any doubt, that I love her. I've

proved my love to her in countless ways through the years. If I need to alter something in my life in order to become what she needs me to become, I do it. If I need to make an adjustment in my attitude about the way I see a certain issue, I make that adjustment. Why? Because I want a lifelong relationship with her — not a disposable one.

The Invitation To Intimacy

Demonstrating love and respect includes remembering that we must never invade our spouse's space for our own benefit. For instance, suppose Linda kept taking money out of my wallet whenever she needed some cash. It would be okay if she did that a couple times. But if she kept doing that, it would become a problem, because she would be invading my personal space.

JUDICIOUS MARRIAGE PARTNERS RARELY INVADE ONE ANOTHER'S SPACE IN ORDER TO *Benefit* THEMSELVES.

Any relationship has unspoken expectations to enter or to remain within it. Therefore, spouses are not to enter each other's space without invitation. Excellence is always mindful of manners and proper protocol; it never invades, even in a relationship as intimate as marriage.

Now, you may say, "Well, Robb, I think you are wrong. Linda should be able to just go in your wallet and take money whenever she needs it." Yes indeed, she should be able to do that, but if she makes a practice of getting into my wallet without permission, she shows disrespect. It is a very simple thing for her to say to me, "Sweetheart, would it be okay if I took this amount of money?" It shows respect. It would be pretty embarrassing for me to put my wallet in my pocket thinking I have money, only to find out later (when it's time to pay for something) that I don't.

We must reenter our marriage relationship every day with respect. We must await the invitation to intimacy, never taking anything for granted. We do this not because we *have* to, but because we *want* to draw our spouse to our daily love affair with them.

Sometimes spouses withdraw from each other because of a need for relational privacy. A husband can shut down (or become emotionally evasive) because he doesn't feel safe enough to be open with his feelings. He needs to know his wife isn't going to judge him or tell him something is wrong with him every time he opens up to her.

A good example is when he comes home at the end of his workday. He needs some space. He needs time to emotionally disconnect from his day and its hustles. The challenge is that his wife also has had a busy day at home or in her work environment. But instead of withdrawing, she wants to talk. So as soon as she sees him, she offloads or dumps the day's problems on him all at once. All that does is cause him frustration.

A wife must learn to wait and let her husband transition and *then* lovingly share her challenges. She must do it in a way that he knows she is not asking him to fix anything, but simply to listen. Sometimes it's even good to say, "Honey, just listen to this — you don't have to do anything about it, but I have to tell you how crazy my day was today." Failure to do this sets the stage for frustration. This is why some husbands just aren't excited about going home.

I had to tell Linda years ago, "Look, I love you, Honey, but I don't need to come home only to be miserable from 5:01 p.m. to bedtime, especially since I still have to deal with everyone else's problems on the telephone!"

"Well, don't you think I face problems too?"

"I understand that you face problems during your day. But to ask me to become an emotional dumping ground for your frustration is to expect me to take God's place in your life. If you're going to continue to expect to receive from me more than I can give, you'll frustrate me and more importantly, you will never be who God called you to be in this marriage."

So give your husband the time he needs to open up and listen to you. He may go into his "cave" and hide for a while, but he'll eventually come out. And when he does, he'll be much more receptive to you than if you offload on him the moment he walks in the door.

⇜ *You Reap What You Sow* ⇝

All of creation, including the institution of marriage, is subject to the Universal Law of Sowing and Reaping. That law is timeless and unchanging; it will be in operation as long as the earth remains. It cannot be broken or overturned in your life. Like the Law of Gravity, the Law of Sowing and Reaping has been perpetually set in motion, and there is nothing we can do to change it.

We have the opportunity to change the course of our marriage by sowing seeds of selflessness and respect. Whatever seeds we sow; whether good or bad, that is the kind of harvest we will reap. Many people say, "It doesn't matter what I do; my marriage will prosper anyway." But that isn't true. Spouses must sow into their marriage *today*, in order to reap a fulfilling relationship in the future.

> MARRIAGES MUST LIVE A *Life of Sowing* TODAY, IN ORDER TO ENJOY REAPING IN THE FUTURE.

Does your spouse behave disrespectfully towards you? Do you know how to get them to start responding positively to you? Start doing right things for them. That's why Jesus said, "Love your enemies. Bless and speak well of those who curse you. Pray for those who despitefully use you" (Matthew 5:44).

Think about it. Suppose a husband wants to be loved, but he keeps judging his wife regarding her lack of love for him.

He wants loyalty in his home, but he's always afraid his wife is cheating on him. He demands monogamy and assurance of undying support and respect.

So how can this husband ensure that his wife loves him and is not cheating on him? First, he has to double up on his love for *her*. He needs to absolutely overpower her with love. Second, he must deal with *himself* in the arena of loyalty, before he demands it of her. He must begin to shut off thoughts that cause his mind to wander away from his home. As he gets rid of his own disloyal thoughts, he opens the way for her to do the same. As he starts sowing these good seeds of love and loyalty, he'll receive a harvest of the same.

So out of your desire to see your spouse give you love and loyalty, you must *first sow* love and loyalty into your spouse. Refuse to allow fear to speak to your mind. Sow, and then trust God. In due season, you will begin to reap a harvest from your seed.

Whenever disloyal thoughts run through my mind, I refuse to allow panic to come upon me. Temptation is not sin. It's simply an attack! So I just double up on my love for my wife, and eventually reap her love in return. It may not happen immediately, but in the end my love will bring out of her what was sown into her life. I know that it's impossible to reap a negative harvest from a consistent sowing of good seed. That's why we must live a life of sowing, in order to enjoy a future of reaping.

This is not simple because we live in the midst of a generation that continually wants to reap. People want to reap personal benefit from their marriage without sowing any good seed for the benefit of their spouse.

Those who operate this way are people of short-term gratification. They don't want to sow into their marriage today, so they can reap long-term rewards in the years ahead. They crave immediate, selfish gratification by focusing only upon what their spouse should do to meet *their* needs.

Proverbs 31 speaks of a spouse who has learned the wisdom of sowing for *long-term* gratification. This woman understands how to sow into her marriage. Verse 12 says, *"She does him good and not evil all the days of her life."* This woman continually sows and sows and sows into her husband's life. She spends her entire life sowing good seed into the lives of those in her family. This is a rare woman who is very secure. As a result, she reaps a great harvest of blessing in her future:

> Her children rise up and call her blessed; her husband also, and he praises her: "Many daughters have done well, but you excel them all."
>
> Proverbs 31:28-29

Remember, excellence takes time. But if you keep plowing the ground and sowing good seed into your marriage, the harvest will come. You won't be able to stop it, because seed sown *always* produces a harvest. It may look like nothing is happening, but I guarantee, you *will* reap blessings in your future when you sow life into your marriage today.

The Law Of Replenished Virtue

Remember the woman with the issue of blood? The Bible says that she came up behind Jesus and pressed through the crowd, telling herself continually, "If I can just touch His garments, I'll be made whole. If I can just touch His garments, I'll be made whole." Finally, she reached Jesus and touched the hem of His garment. At that moment, virtue came into her, and she knew she had been healed of the plague.

Jesus knew that power had gone out of Him, through the touch of faith. He looked around and asked, "Who touched Me?"

His disciples laughed and asked, "What do You mean, Jesus? Everyone is pressing in on You and touching You."

"No, you don't understand," Jesus replied.

Life or virtue was actually drawn out of Jesus at that moment, and He had to respond! When the woman came forth and gave her testimony, Jesus was revived.

This demonstrates *the law of replenished virtue* in operation. It's important for you to understand this law, especially if you both make a practice of pursuing the success of other people. As you minister to others (including your children), life and virtue are constantly drawn out of you, and you both must continually replenish each other.

So when our spouse comes to the end of the day feeling depleted from the day's interactions with other people, we need to be sensitive enough to detect how they are feeling. When they seem irritated from a hard day's work, look for ways to replenish the virtue that has been drained out, by sowing life back into them.

Full-time ministry can be exhausting. After a full day of preaching or counseling, I tend to become introspective. I may pull away to be by myself; I may even cry. Why? Because once a person has been under the anointing of God for a period of time and it lifts, he or she experiences a low. Sometimes I feel like, "Lord, I'd give everything to be under that anointing for two more minutes."

That's why, when people want to come up for fellowship after I've ministered, I often don't want to talk. Then I begin to deal with my shortcomings. I think about things I didn't say. *God, I should have told them this. This would have really helped them, Lord.* I pray for the people, asking God to help them hear His voice.

By the time I get home, I feel completely drained. It's such a blessing when Linda is right there to greet me and to pour life back into me with loving words of encouragement and support.

It's so important that we understand this law of replenished virtue — because we will continually be called upon to be sowers of life into our marriage partners, when they feel depleted and drained.

∾ Completing One Another ∾

But how can we do this unless we learn how to appreciate our spouse for who they are, instead of penalizing them for who they are not?

A number of years ago, a church consultant came and spent several days talking to my staff members. Afterward, he said to me, "You know, you're amazing."

"What do you mean?" I asked. I was just waiting for him to tell me all the things I needed to change in the way I ran the church. Instead, the consultant remarked, "I've never seen anyone who was able, so successfully, to assemble a church staff in such a way that it covered his own shortcomings. You have staffed to your weaknesses extremely well!"

Loving PARTNERS POSTURE THEMSELVES TO COMPENSATE FOR THE WEAKNESS OF THEIR MATE.

It is natural to want to surround ourselves with people who are similar to us, rather than different. We are often intimidated by people who have strengths that we don't have. It is critical to learn how to staff your life in such a way that you compensate for what you lack.

The gifts and skills that God has not given to *you* are hidden in the life of someone around you. This is especially true of your spouse. He or she has strengths you don't have. Likewise, you have gifts and strengths your spouse doesn't have. This is why you both must posture yourselves to fill in the gaps where the other is weak. You are to complete one another. This is the simplest definition of the God-kind of marriage.

The Power Of Gratitude

When you are thankful, your spouse will continually be drawn to give to you. Why is that? There is tremendous fulfillment in seeing the demonstration of a grateful heart!

Nothing gives me more joy than to see Linda happy and thankful. I cannot express just how happy it makes me feel to see her walking around whistling and singing. It blesses me when she walks by and says spontaneously from her heart, "You know, Honey, you're the greatest!"

When your husband knows you are at peace and grateful for all he does for you, he starts looking for more ways to bless you. He looks forward to coming home and walking in the door every night to a wife who hugs him and tells him how important he is to her; how glad she is to be married to him; and how thankful she is that he's decided to lay down his life for her.

> *Gratitude* CREATES THE DESIRE IN YOUR SPOUSE TO GIVE YOU EVEN MORE.

Remember — there was a reason Samson wanted Delilah. **She understood how to please him** (though her motives were not in his best interest). It is very easy for a man to cherish and take care of a wife like that, because gratitude always creates a desire in a spouse's heart to give even more.

Husbands, I know that it's often not easy to express (or even to *remember* to express!) the loving thoughts you hold in your heart towards your wife. But when you come home to a woman who has invested her whole day and her whole heart into taking care of *your* needs and the needs of your family, even just a *little* gratitude will go a long way! Recognize her contributions. If seeing *her* happy is what makes *you* happy, be generous in expressing your gratitude and appreciation for all that she does. A treasured, appreciated wife is a happy wife!

This principle describes the way married life should be all the time. You should continually respect each other, love each other, and show one another how much you care. Every shared moment needs to be embraced, savored, and cherished. You never really know if today's time together will be your last time together.

I know it takes *faith* to be a good husband or a good wife. But from this day forward, you can start moving toward that goal. You can make the most of every moment, as you sow life into your spouse and receive life in return. Your marriage relationship can become all that God has called it to be — a reflection of His love for His bride, the church.

Make the choice to become the best marriage partner you can be. You're in it for the long haul. Trust in God, love your spouse, and get into the Word. God will show you how to make things better in every aspect of your relationship, as you cast off mediocrity and head toward a truly *excellent* marriage.

CHAPTER PRINCIPLES

- The right marriage partners know when they entered marriage, they did it for their spouse, not for themselves.

- Devoted marriage partners maintain a consistent willingness to change for the benefit of their spouse.

- Learn the art of diffusing potential problems before they start.

- An understanding marriage partner never responds to an attitude with an attitude.

- The way you treat your spouse is the way you believe God treats you.

- Judicious marriage partners rarely invade one another's space in order to benefit themselves.

- Marriages must live a life of sowing today, in order to enjoy a life of reaping in the future.

- Loving partners posture themselves to compensate for the weaknesses of their mate.

- Gratitude creates the desire in your spouse to give you even more.

- Live every day as though it were your last day together.

CHAPTER 5

Nuptial Needs

Let's be honest. Sometimes the words "I'm in it for the long haul" can sound like a prison sentence, served behind the bars of a marriage contract. Marriage was God's first and most beautiful institution, and it *can* be the most glorious experience we ever get to enjoy. But, as countless couples have discovered through the ages, it also can be a most challenging experience, if we don't do it God's way.

Blended Lives

When we first start dating our prospective mate, we enjoy one another's company so much that we just don't know how we could ever live a day without seeing each other. Before I got married, I only saw Linda when I wanted to — and I wanted to almost all the time!

You probably felt the same way. But after you got married, you began to share *everything* together, the bathroom, the housework, the bills, and so on. Before you were married, she really liked the fact that you never wanted to watch television; you just wanted to focus on her. She didn't realize that it wasn't that you didn't watch TV *at all*. You just watched it away from her, in the wee hours of the morning!

So now that you're together, perhaps you've found out things aren't quite so illustrious. Your married life doesn't seem to be "shining ever brighter unto the perfect day" (*see* Proverbs 4:18)!

If that describes your marriage, your case is not unusual. People who have been married for a little while often tend to get a little cynical. But if they're not careful, the spark they had in the beginning begins to dwindle as time goes by. Once the romance goes out of their marriage, it becomes easy for them to start fantasizing about romance. The problem is, their marriage partner is usually *not* the one they fantasize about! As a result, these marriage partners start hiding their real selves from each other; thus, love begins to slowly die.

But there is a way to keep that from happening to you. You can have not just a good marriage, but one that is a testimony to the world. You can keep that spark vibrant and alive, as you and your spouse fulfill your responsibilities before God, allowing Him to continually change you into new people. So take heart!

Allow me to share some important keys that can help you and your spouse not only feel comfortable in your marriage, but spark an excitement within you to go even deeper into your relationship. I'm going to show you how to fall in love day after day, after day, after day, with that special person you married.

The Treasure Is Buried In A Field

We fall in love by choice, not by chance. Success in marriage doesn't necessarily depend on passing a compatibility test before you get married. Rather, *success in marriage is completely dependent on how willing you both are to meet each other's needs.*

When you read God's Word, you read about ideal perfection — the way things are supposed to be. Then, when you take your eyes out of the Word of God, you begin to see the way life presents itself to you. You begin to see the person to whom you're married and the problems he or she has. How you respond to your mate's imperfections lets you know whether you're in love with *the person* you married or merely with *the idea* of getting married. Remember, when you made those wedding vows, you committed yourself to an imperfect human being.

> ACCEPT THE FACT THAT WHEN YOU GOT *The Treasure* YOU BOUGHT THE FIELD.

This reminds me of the parable Jesus related in Matthew 13:44 about the treasure hidden in a field. The man who found the buried treasure covered it up again; then he went and sold everything he owned in order to buy not just the treasure, but also the entire field.

Well, even though my wife is no doubt convinced of the fact that I am a great treasure, she didn't just buy the treasure when she married me — she bought the field. She has to put up with all my imperfections, faults, and idiosyncrasies. There are certain aspects of me — my tastes, my moods — that aren't like hers. For instance, there are certain foods I enjoy that she absolutely doesn't. Nevertheless, that's part of the field Linda bought when she got her treasure called Robb!

Modern society doesn't teach this concept to people, so most married couples don't understand that they got the entire field when they bought their "treasure." That's why so many distorted ideas about marriage and commitment swirl around in the world today.

I certainly had wrong ideas about marriage before I was born again. In fact, I thought marriage was something you could just throw away if you didn't like it. If you find someone who looks good, I reasoned, you should go ahead and marry her. If it doesn't work out, you can always get a divorce and try again later.

Where did I get such wrong ideas about marriage? Well, I never had an example of a good marriage from which to learn when I was growing up. My mom and dad weren't Christians. They didn't know what it meant to be married, nor did they know how to truly love one another.

Wrong ideas about marriage are rampant in today's world, even in the church. We constantly read reports of prominent men and women of God who are actually looking for reasons to get their marriages annulled. Though they run large church denominations, they want to find a way to escape their marriage commitments and still look respectable.

There is one lady who had been married for thirty-two years and had seven children. When her husband decided he did not want to have any more children, she got an annulment. How tragic! She wasn't willing to work on her marriage. She was filled with selfishness. And that woman is just one of millions of people who think the same way about marriage.

Every great marriage becomes great only because the two partners continually *do what it takes* to make it great. They spend time speaking God's Word over their marriage. They invest the necessary time to develop a give-and-take relationship. They have learned to be ever ready to believe the best of each other.

A Giving Marriage

Here is a dynamic principle: **Great marriages are built by great givers.** Both partners have to learn how to truly love one another according to God's Word.

Contrary to popular opinion, when you get married you don't automatically live happily ever after. In fact, if you or your spouse refuses to change wrong attitudes after you get married, you won't live happily at all!

As we discussed earlier, marriage isn't something you enter into in order to become complete or to get something you don't have within yourself. Marriage is supposed to be a covenant relationship in which two people learn how to *complement* one another, like a hand fitting into a glove. This kind of marriage is achieved when both marriage partners maintain a sense of compassion for one another. They forgive and overlook each other's "field" — their faults and their shortcomings — on a daily basis. Then they choose to live passionately for each other.

True Affection

So what are the basic needs of marriage partners? Well, the first need of the wife is affection — *without* sex. Husbands, you've been taking from her since the day you met her. Learn how to *give into* her life.

Your wife needs you to put your arm around her, even when you don't want anything. She needs you to hold her hand, to pull her closer to you as you sit together on the sofa or church pew.

Show your wife that she's as important to you *today* as she was when you first got married. Show her that you care for her now as much as you ever did. She needs to be held. She needs to be loved. She needs to be cared for. She needs to be given the security of closeness and intimacy without sex.

ABUNDANT *Affection* IS AN IMPORTANT KEY TO A HARMONIOUS HOME.

I know that's a difficult challenge for us as husbands, because we're geared in one direction—the physical act of sex.

Let me say this to you husbands: We don't think the way our wives do. But if we fail to show our wives the affection they need, we'll sabotage our sexual relationship with them. They'll start telling us, "The only thing you ever want is sex!"

Our wives are not legal prostitutes for us, and affection isn't just the prelude to a sexual encounter. Lovemaking doesn't start when we go to bed at night. Lovemaking starts with a consistent demonstration of affection that begins when we open our eyes in the morning.

So find ways throughout the day to show affection to your wife, through a gentle touch or a loving word. Tell her that your desire is to be with her. Tell her how much she means to you. Tell her that you're excited to go out every day and be a winner, so you can bring home to her the increase from the work of your hands. Tell her how much she excites and pleases you.

That's how you create a desire in your wife to come near to you. That's how you kindle a flame in her that never burns out! That is how you enhance her sexual attraction to you.

Sex

It is said that men are 90% sexual and 10% emotional, whereas women are 90% emotional and 10% sexual. *Men and women are different!*

Wives, if you were to go to your husband and say, "Baby, what do you need? What can I do for you?"— You probably have a pretty good idea what he would say! The first thing that would come to his mind is *sexual fulfillment*. You may have already realized that! But don't think, "Oh, that's just the way he is. It's just a characteristic of the male species." That isn't true.

In fact, the wife is the one who actually sets the sexual temperature of her home. If she has a bad attitude about making love to her husband, he will avoid her. And even when he doesn't, he'll just come and get what he wants and not think about her needs.

That doesn't mean the husband doesn't love his wife. The fact is that most men are considerate concerning the physical relationship with their wives.

If a husband has any kind of heart at all, he will not continually push himself on his wife. He will allow her to go her own way. If the wife shows no interest in him, she gets no interest back from him. Consequently, the marriage relationship begins to suffer.

Eventually the devil will find an opening to say to the husband, "Look, what about that young woman down at the office? She is always willing to hear you out. She's understanding. She's loving. She's respectful. She wants to be taken care of." If the husband isn't careful, he'll begin to share some of his frustrations with her. Soon she'll seem to be everything his wife isn't. He won't find out until after he breaks up his home and marries the other woman, that she is no different that his ex-wife.

> AN IMPORTANT *Ingredient* TO FIDELITY IN THE HOME IS TO NEVER ALLOW SEX TO BECOME ROUTINE

First Corinthians 7:2 says, *"Nevertheless, because of sexual immorality, let each man have his own wife, and let each woman have her own husband."* When a husband and wife stop having a regular physical relationship with one another, their bodies eventually shut down to passion and desire. Soon the wife lives in a house with a man who doesn't really care about anything; he just pays the bills.

The true temperature of your marriage can be measured by the amount of time you spend together physically. So, wives, continually prepare yourself mentally and emotionally for the next time you make love to your husband. Think about how you can hardly wait for him to come home. Think about how you want to please him, to love him, to be with him. Keep him from ever looking for excitement anywhere else!

⌒ *Communication* ⌒

The second basic need of the wife is *conversation*. Women need conversation, and a marriage needs communication. In fact, I once asked the late Dr. Lester Sumrall, "What is the most important thing a couple can do for their marriage?"

Dr. Sumrall replied, *"They need to talk to each other."*

MEANINGFUL *Communication* IS A REQUIREMENT, NOT AN OPTION.

When a husband and wife continually converse with each other, they form an ever-closer bond between them. That should always be their goal, because God didn't call them to live two separate lives in one house.

"Well, she does her thing, and I do mine." No, that doesn't work when you're trying to build an exceptional marriage. You're supposed to be a team. If you aren't a team, it is only a matter of time before your marriage doesn't have any players!

Husbands, ask your wife how you're doing in this area of communication. If she is like countless other women, she doesn't think you talk to her enough about what is going on in your life. She might also say that you don't *really listen* when she is trying to communicate with you. It isn't enough for you to *hear* her so your eardrum vibrates; she needs you to actually *listen* to her and to make her feel like her conversation has value to you.

Now, I am personally not a very good conversationalist. I often have to force myself to converse with people. So by the time I get home, I think that I've already said it all, and that Linda already knows everything I've said.

And I'm not alone. To my remembrance, I've never heard a man say, "I wish my wife would communicate with me more." If it were up to me, I would use the shortest possible responses I can use; "Yes"; "No"; "Maybe"; "A little bit"; and "I don't know." And if the wife wants more than that, husbands typically think, "Gosh, what is she looking for — an Encyclopedia Britannica?"

However, wives, let me address you for a moment. *True communication is a two-way street.* Let's talk about misunderstandings for a moment. I've found that the number-one reason for miscommunication is lack of definition of terms. What do I mean? Your words don't always communicate what you want to say. In other words, what you say to me might be different than what you *mean to say.*

That's why it's important that we always *define our terms* when communicating with each other. I may stop you as you're talking and say, "Tell me what you mean." You may think, "Well, you know what that word means." But have you considered than although I know what it means to *me*, I don't know what it means to *you*! I want to find out what it means to *you*, so I can be sure that I am communicating what I mean to communicate.

You may want to please your spouse and do what is right in your marriage. You may want to be such a blessing to him or her that he or she would never desire to be married to anyone else in the world. However, if you don't know how to truly meet each other's needs, all your good intentions won't produce the right results.

That has happened more than once in my marriage. I'll ask Linda to do something, and she will go out and do it according to what she heard me say. She wasn't wrong in what she heard; she and I just have a different set of definitions for certain terms.

To make matters worse, I'd get upset when Linda did something for me differently than what I expected, and she'd say to me, "Well, I was only trying to do what you asked me to do for you!"

This happens all the time in marriages, many times on a daily basis. A wife often comes to the place where she no longer wants to serve in her marriage, because she's continually being told that she didn't do things right. All her efforts never seem to satisfy or please her husband, so she thinks, "Why should I even try anymore? I'm no good at anything!"

But this downward spiral in marriage never has to take place. Spouses must seek to *understand* as well as *to be understood* when needs are communicated.

The bottom line is this, husbands: *Your successful communication with your wife is based on a correct and mutually agreed upon definition of terms*. Understand this principle, and you will avoid countless unnecessary pitfalls in your marriage.

It's also important to understand that different individuals communicate in different ways. A person's childhood environment often comes into play here. Perhaps your husband comes from a home where no one knew how to effectively communicate. Maybe your wife's father was hardly ever home, so there was never enough time for her to talk to her father the way she longed to. All these things can affect how a person communicates with his or her spouse.

Actually, there is no right way or wrong way to communicate. There is no set amount of time that you and your wife must spend talking to each other in order to spend "enough" time. You've communicated the "right way," and you've spent "enough" time when both of you make a connection and feel that you have truly been *heard and understood*.

This is an area with which men have a tough time. Wives need to be understanding. They should be careful not to place unrealistic expectations on their husbands. Most men have not been prepared and equipped for effective communication. This is the number one complaint of women.

If you are having communication issues with your husband, you may need to find another woman to be that best friend you're looking for. Don't pressure your husband to be something more than he is capable of right now in your life.

Let me tell you something about your man, so you can

understand him a little better. It isn't easy for him to fulfill this need of yours. I don't know how to do it myself, but I'm working on it! Men typically *don't know how* to hear their wife's voice, listen to her plight, acknowledge her input as having worth — but then, out of obedience to God, do something different than what she requests.

I've been caught, many times, in the trap of becoming what other people needed, even when it wasn't what I believed God wanted me to do. Although I did this because I wanted those individuals to know they had worth, I now believe it was a mistake.

It sometimes seems as if we settle for one extreme or the other in life. Either we become what everyone else wants us to be, or we become what others perceive as a big "ogre" — someone who always pushes for his own way, who always declares, "We're going to do it this way, bless God! That's just the way it is!" Frankly, I'm still trying to find the right balance between those two extremes. But that's why marriage drives us all straight into faith — because, in our own natural strength, we can't do what God called us to do!

Companionship

A wife's need for conversation corresponds with her husband's need for *companionship*. He needs you to want to be around him and to do things with him that he enjoys.

Personally, I don't like traveling without Linda. Of course,

I realize there are times when she just can't go along with me. But I like it very much when she can!

For what does a husband look in the arena of companionship? Well, first let me tell you what he does *not* look for. He does not look for a cook, a second mother, or a conscience! And it might not always look like it, but when it comes right down to it, he does not look for a sexual partner.

The husband looks for someone to walk with him through the situations of life. He looks for someone to believe in him and give undying loyalty to him. He looks for someone for whom he can be a champion—a hero!

> SECURITY IS BIRTHED THE MOMENT YOU PROVIDE *Loyal* AND *Loving* COMPANIONSHIP.

A wife who fulfills her role as a loving, loyal companion is a priceless treasure to her husband. Do you know why? Because people *pretend* they want to please him every second of the day, for money or favors. They tell him what a great guy he is, for a few bucks. But what he really wants is someone who esteems him and wants to please him *just because of her love for him*.

Why would I ever want a secretary or some other woman to fulfill my need for companionship? That woman would only do it because she doesn't know all my quirks and idiosyncrasies. But I have a woman at home who knows me intimately and *still* remains my most loyal supporter and steadfast companion!

Women often look at me and marvel, "Oh, he's just so wonderful. He must be such a great husband!"

I tell them, "You know what? You wouldn't be able to handle me! You'd think I was on your case every day, as I made certain you did what it took to help me fulfill what I'm called to do. You couldn't take living with me — but Linda can! She's just the companion I need!"

That's how every husband should feel about his wife!

Transparency

The third basic need of the wife is *honesty and openness*. Husbands, she needs you to be *lovingly* (not judgmentally) honest and open with her. Remember, your wife is a treasure to be handled with gentleness and compassion. Always keep discretion and tact in mind, when communicating honestly.

> BE LOVINGLY HONEST, NURTURING, AND *Transparent* AT ALL TIMES.

Now, being honest and open doesn't mean you should get yourself in trouble by thinking, "Well, that's it — I'm going to tell her about every sexually tempting thought I've had for ten years." No — don't just jump in and make a mess of things! You need to start with the small issues and let your openness with her grow from there. However, realize that *your wife wants to know you.* Therefore, she needs you to constantly work toward becoming more open and more honest than you've ever been before.

I speak to so many women who have no idea what their husbands are really like. For instance, many wives have no clue about how much money is in their bank accounts, because their husbands keep them away from all the family finances.

I recently ministered to a woman who had been doing very well in business, before she got married a few years ago. Now she and her husband owe more than $300,000 in unsecured debt. This woman just wanted to help her new husband realize his dream, but ultimately she only succeeded in deeply hurting her own sense of security. That is a marriage that is greatly lacking in transparency or openness.

However, here's an important point for every wife to consider: Although a wife needs truth and openness from her husband, at the same time she has to be *ready* for truth. That's where the third need of the husband comes into play.

Unconditional Acceptance

On the flip side of a wife's need for her husband to be honest and open with her is the husband's need for her acceptance and approval whenever he *is* honest and open.

Wives, you need to accept your husband's honesty without trying to use what he tells you to control or manipulate him. How can you use your husband's words against him? By refusing to show unconditional acceptance of him when he is honest with you. Your disapproval of him may begin to work on him little by little, until eventually he yields and you get your way. You may think that's a good outcome, but it's actually a sure way to keep the husband from being honest and open again!

Acceptance AND APPROVAL ARE ALWAYS THE REWARD FOR TRANSPARENCY.

Another reason some husbands aren't open with their wives is that their wives react so negatively every time they try to be open. Contrary to popular opinion, most men don't like to argue. That's not how they normally resolve conflict.

If two men get angry at each other, they may say, "Shut your mouth or I'll knock your teeth out!" But once they blow off steam, the conflict is over. They shake hands, slap each other on the back, and go out for lunch together.

On the other hand, women usually want to talk, and talk, and talk to resolve a conflict. And even when the argument is over, it's often *not* over for the woman. So the husband is often reluctant to be honest and open with his wife, because he doesn't want to raise questions in her mind that will start an extended argument. He knows there will be thirty more questions he can't answer, after he tells her the truth.

With this in mind, what is the best way for you to respond

when your husband is open and honest with you? You should just listen and be understanding. As Proverbs 19:14 (TLB) says, *"A father can give his sons homes and riches, but only the Lord can give them understanding wives."*

An understanding wife creates a nonjudgmental atmosphere in her home and thus causes communication to become fluent between her and her husband. The moment the home atmosphere becomes judgmental, he begins to close up; he can no longer tell his wife about his dreams and goals. But when she creates a harbor of peace, she becomes *an anchor for his future instead of a judge of his failures.*

A wife assumes the role of judge when she says to her husband, "This is what I think you should do." And just as Adam lost God's best in order to please Eve, that husband risks making the same mistake, by trying to please his wife instead of doing what he believes the Lord wants him to do.

That is the reason a wife has to learn to create a nonjudgmental atmosphere for her husband. She should never make him afraid to talk to her.

If the man in a woman's life becomes silent, he is probably afraid of how she'll react if he talks to her. If this situation continues, he may eventually go find another woman to whom he *can* talk. He never actually wanted to stop talking; he just wanted to share his heart without being judged.

So maintain an atmosphere in your home that invites your husband to be open with you. When he talks, *listen* to him, in an atmosphere of acceptance and approval, without always interrupting with your input. As you are faithful to do that, your husband will come to the place where he *loves* to talk to you!

Financial Security

Husbands, your wife needs financial security. She should never have to think, "Oh, my Lord, what are we going to do? We have all these bills! How are we going to pay them?" Don't put her underneath the burden of those bills. Don't make her think she has to go get a job so the bills can be paid. Your wife should never *have to* work.

IN MARRIAGE, NEVER UNDERESTIMATE THE POWER OF *Money*.

Let me say something to the husband who is married to a homemaker. What she does at home is more than what you do at the workplace. I mean, you might go sit on the forklift all day long, but she's at home lifting all the little bambinos you gave her! She changes the diapers that you don't want to change. She goes to the PTA meetings that you want nothing to do with. Then you come home and ask her, "Well, what have you been doing all day? You don't have anything to do! You're just on marital welfare!"

You need to make it your aim to keep your wife feeling

financially secure. "But I don't make enough money," you may say. Well, then, do one of two things. Change jobs, or lower your lifestyle until you do make more money!

What benefit is there in owning a bigger house, if neither of you are ever there to enjoy it because you're both always working? What benefit is there in owning a lot of material possessions, if your wife has to work outside the home against her own wishes?

When you and your wife are both working so hard that you hardly ever see each other, you open up yourself to temptation. And if divorce is the result, your pursuit of material gain just gave you more things to fight over and to split up between the two of you!

Personally, I believe that a wife should not work outside the home unless it's absolutely necessary, especially when the children are small. If anything, she can work at home, in her free time, to make a little extra income. That's why home-based businesses are becoming very popular now — because mothers *want* to spend time with their children, and children *need* to spend time with their mothers.

Once the children are well into high school or out on their own, that's the time for the wife to think about going back to work or becoming more involved in volunteer work for her church or for a charitable organization. For instance, she could visit the sick or go to nursing homes and visit the elderly. She could also get involved in prison ministry, go back to school, and so on.

If the couple decides at that time that they want to buy a new home, a new car, or other extras, the wife might want to go back to work to make sure they stay out of debt, as they enjoy this season of their lives. Nevertheless, **the husband remains the one who is primarily responsible for bringing in the family income.**

I believe the notion that the wife can just as easily be the primary breadwinner is one of the travesties of the modern age. But I can tell you how that notion began to gain acceptance in today's society. It started with the big push to make husbands and wives equal in the decision-making process within a marriage.

Husbands began to say, "Well, if you're going to be equal in the decision-making process, then you're going to be equal in the money-making process too." Then wives began to say, "If I'm going to be responsible for making money, you're not going to make the decisions about how I spend it."

That's when married couples started using two checkbooks. And now, more and more frequently, I hear couples say things such as, "Well, he pays the rent and the utilities, and I pay for all the other family expenses." I ask them, "How can you two call yourselves married?" Many modern couples have created such a separated existence that they've almost reached a state of legalized cohabitation!

Christians need to leave behind all these worldly ideas

about marriage and get back to God's way. Within the divine design for the covenant of marriage, God built inside of the woman the need for financial security. This is a need that the wife should not have to struggle to fulfill. Again, it is *the husband's responsibility and his privilege* to provide for his family through the work of his own hands.

Domestic Support

Next, let's talk about the husband's need for *domestic support*. This has to do with keeping the house clean, making sure his clothes are clean and pressed, and so on.

I get reports from husbands all the time whose wives lie around all day and never do anything to keep up the home. However, the husbands can't say anything about it to their wives, because when they do, the wives make them pay for it dearly!

I've been in the homes of some very well known ministers where the husband is looking all over the house for a sock, or the wife casually says, "Oops! I forgot to iron your shirt." I can't help but sit there and think, "You need to live what you preach, wife!"

> *Support*, NOT CONTROL, IS ALL A SPOUSE NEEDS TO ACHIEVE THEIR DREAMS.

Why? Because those of us who are ministers are called by God to raise the standard of our surroundings to the level at which we preach. That's why my house is always clean. We don't live with things strewn all over the place.

For the most part, my wife takes care of our home all by herself — and we have a fairly large home! I cannot understand wives who stay home all day and think they have to hire a housekeeper and a nanny for their three children!

Of course, I understand that each family's situation is different. You just have to deal with whatever is on your plate, the best way you know how. For instance, if a wife works long hours, either in a home-based business or outside the home, she needs help from the husband and children to keep the house clean. Even if she's an at-home mother, the husband can still pitch in and help at times. He can tell the children, "Mommy planned to do this for you, but I'm going to do it today because I want to be with you." Whatever the situation is in your home, stay positive, so that the children keep a healthy attitude about helping around the house and about marriage in general.

Personally, I help around the house all the time. I spend much of my time at home, whereas Linda spends a lot of time at the office. I've found that if I go to the office, I don't get a lot accomplished, because people constantly come to me, asking for a little of my time.

So when I need to spend time studying, praying, emailing, and making critical decisions, I usually do it at home. And while I walk around our home, I straighten up the house. It isn't that Linda expects me to do this. I do it because I *want* to.

Also, Linda gets up before me, so I'm the one who makes the bed. Every morning, without fail, my bed is made within thirty seconds of the time I get out of it. I help keep the rest of the bedroom clean, too. The door to our bedroom stays open, and friends tell me it always looks like something out of a home interior magazine!

The wife also provides domestic support to the husband by making sure the children understand that Daddy is the boss.

Wives need to make their children feel like their dad is the fourth member of the Trinity! Why? Because too often the demands of work prevent husbands from enjoying much fellowship with their families, as they watch their children grow up.

That's why one of the greatest things you can ever do to meet your husband's need for domestic support is to build up his image in the eyes of the children. Your children will believe about their father whatever you tell them. He usually cannot spend as much time with them as you do, so it's important that you speak often of their dad's admirable qualities.

When the children think of their dad, they should think, "My dad loves me. My dad is working hard, making money so we can have a nice house. My dad loves me so much, he's letting me go to this school." These are the kinds of things you should teach your children about their father!

But what will happen if you walk around complaining

about your husband all the time? What if you often argue with him in front of the children? What if you always take the children's side when they disagree with their dad's decisions? There will be a breakdown in your children's understanding of a healthy marriage relationship. They will grow up to one day challenge their own spouse, and they will sow their own disappointments into the hearts of their children.

So if you ever have a problem with your husband, *don't* deal with it in front of your kids, and *don't* talk to them about it. Your children are not your counselors! They are not your best friends either!

I have a friend whose mother always told the children, "When Dad comes home, I want the home to be quiet and peaceful, and you should have all your homework done." This mother provided the domestic support her husband needed. She consistently built into her children an image of their dad that generated a deep sense of respect and love for him.

To this day, every one of the children in that family has grown up to be successful in his or her chosen field. That's the mark of a good wife!

Commitment To Family

The last need of the wife that we're going to discuss is *family commitment*. Husbands, your wife needs to spend time with her family — her parents, her siblings, and so forth.

Now, honestly, I don't really understand *why* she needs that time with her family. I just know it's a need that most men don't have.

You'll hardly ever find a female hermit. All the hermits of this world are men! When women get together, they all hug and talk, talk, *talk*. When they get together with family members, they hug when they get there; they hug while they're there; and they hug when they leave! And while the wife fellowships all day long, the husband falls asleep from boredom!

> *Commitment*
> TO THE FAMILY IS AN EMOTIONAL WORK OF ART, ON DISPLAY FOR ALL TO SEE.

He says to her, "Hey, can we go now? Come on, let's go!"

She replies, "Oh, come on, just a little while longer."

The kids plead, "Oh, Dad, let us stay! Please, let's stay a little longer!"

And the husband thinks, "My Lord, all I've been doing here is sleeping or watching sports on television all day long!"

Many men just don't have that same deep need for family connection that women do. They can go to their own house and just stay happily by themselves. Every once in a while, they might look out the window to make sure no one is coming down their block to visit. Their motto? "My house is my castle!"

But women are different than men (not better or worse — just different!). They love to visit their loved ones and fellowship with them. They love to play games together.

So the wife might say to the husband, "You never want to do anything with the family."

The husband thinks to himself, "I don't know what to do!" So he says to his wife, "Let's do what *you* want to do."

"Well, I don't want to do what *I* want to do. I want to do what *you* want to do."

The husband thinks, "But I don't want to do anything!"

I've certainly lived through similar scenarios in times past. Let me tell you something about myself: In the areas of life for which I *know* I'm responsible, don't get in my way — I know exactly what to do. But in areas I *don't* know about, such as planning family time, I'll just admit, "I don't know anything about this. It isn't that I don't *want* to have anything to do with it; it's just that *I don't know how*. I'm not that smart!"

I don't think about playing Scrabble with the in-laws or about playing Monopoly with the kids. I think about, "Man, we need another bedroom," or "I wonder what our fuel costs will be this winter." Sadly, we men often haven't been taught the fact that we *are* responsible for establishing strong, intimate ties of commitment within our families — so we end up focusing on other things, while expecting our wives to pick up our slack in this arena.

I do understand that my wife needs time with her siblings and with her parents, so I try to make sure she has that time. What if the wife's family lives out of state? Then the husband needs to provide enough income for her to spend at least a few days a year with her family. Now, of course, the husband also needs to honor *his* parents, but he doesn't have that same need to spend a lot of time with them.

Marriage involves a woman leaving her family and giving up her name to cleave to a man. Because of her psychological makeup, she has a deep need to connect; therefore she also perceives disconnection very differently. She needs time to return to the family she loves for a visit. The children also need a sense of heritage and relationship with their extended family — something both the father and the mother should provide.

Respect

The number-one need of a man is to be respected. Men need unconditional respect in the same way that women need unconditional love. I am not talking about irresponsible men. I mean learning to respect your husband even when he doesn't bring in sufficient funds or he gets fired from his job.

When I walk in my house, I don't want to be immediately told, "Oh, hey, the garbage is over there. You need to take it out and dump it. Oh, and by the way, the bills are on the counter."

MUTUAL *Respect* TOPS THE LIST FOR A MARRIAGE THAT LASTS A LIFETIME.

That's the kind of greeting far too many men get when they come home from work. Life goes from morning until night without any celebration of Dad. There is nothing said about "Isn't Dad great?" or "Aren't we thankful for how hard he works?" Instead of saying, "Let's pray for Daddy right now. He has to work late tonight," Mom says, "Dad is working late *again*."

God's Word tells us that the husband needs to be respected. Ephesians 5:33 says, "*...let the wife see that she respects her husband.*" You may say, "Well, respect has to be earned." But notice this verse *doesn't* say "Let the wife see that she respects her husband *when he deserves that respect.*"

I believe it's true that respect will be much easier for the wife to give if her husband acts respectable. But if he doesn't, that doesn't change God's command to her.

As my wife, Linda needs to respect me. She doesn't respect me only when I act respectable. She respects me because God told her to respect me.

The truth of the matter is that respect isn't created when the receiver fulfills certain requirements. Respect is derived from the grace of the giver. For instance, even if a person hasn't acted respectable and has wrecked his life, I can still treat him with respect. I know there is some good quality in that person's life for which he was never recognized, and for that I can respect him.

Wives should never let a day go by without demonstrating respect to their husbands. If you're not careful, you'll allow your reverence and respect for him to slip. A day will turn into a week; a week will turn into a month; a month will turn into a cold, hard year, and your husband will still be waiting for the woman God gave him to fill his need for respect and appreciation.

Remember, the Universal Law of Sowing and Reaping is foundational to your marriage relationship. If you desire more love, you must first sow more love. If you crave more respect, you must first be more respectful. If you have needs that are not getting met, begin to *extravagantly* meet the needs of your spouse. It won't be long before *both* of you are happy and fulfilled, and your marriage is flourishing!

CHAPTER PRINCIPLES

- Accept the fact that when you got the treasure, you bought the field.

- Abundant affection is an important key to a harmonious home.

- An important ingredient to fidelity in the home is to never allow sex to become routine.

- Meaningful communication is a requirement, not an option.

- Security is birthed the moment you provide loving and loyal companionship.

- Be *lovingly* honest, nurturing, and transparent at all times.

- Acceptance and approval are always the reward for transparency.

- In marriage, never underestimate the power of money.

- Support, not control, is all a spouse needs to achieve their dreams.

- Commitment to the family is an emotional work of art, on display for all to see.

- Mutual respect tops the list for a marriage that lasts a lifetime.

A Final Note

Make it your aim to walk in the love of God toward each other — the love that *"...does not insist on its own rights or its own way, for it is not self-seeking..."* (1 Corinthians 13:5, AMP). Remember — marriage can be the most glorious or the most horrendous experience of your life. The quality of life you and your spouse enjoy together depends completely on your willingness to meet each other's needs.

Too many spouses start looking for the exit door when their marriage relationship becomes difficult. The divorce option is too readily available and too often utilized. Remember, marriage is a covenant — and the essence of covenant is, "I will never leave."

If you are not happy with the present condition of your marriage, I urge you to completely exhaust all other options before you even consider a divorce. Go stand in front of a mirror, and get thoroughly honest with yourself. Ask yourself, "How have I contributed to the difficulty we are having? What changes can I make to see our relationship improve? Am I willing to unselfishly *change*, and to scripturally fulfill *my role* in this marriage, despite what my spouse decides to do?"

My hope is that this book gives you a Biblical pattern to follow to improve your marriage relationship. As you and your spouse implement the tools that I've shared with you, you can build a happy, fulfilling, and lasting marriage, the way Heaven designed it!

Prayer of Commitment

If you want to live in your marriage God's way instead of the world's way, pray this prayer from your heart:

Father, I ask You to forgive me for allowing the generation in which I live to change the way You want me to view the most special person in my life. In the Name of Jesus, I ask that You change me. Slow me down, Lord. Cause me to be swift to hear and slow to speak, to be softhearted, to give soft answers, and in every way possible, to be a blessing to my spouse. Teach me how to please rather than to always expect to be pleased.

I make a quality decision right now to never take authority over something for which You haven't given me responsibility, and I roll the whole of my care regarding my marriage on You. Make me everything You have called me to be, Lord. I thank You for working Your perfect will in both me and my spouse. In Jesus' Name. Amen.

Other Great Books by
Dr. Robb D. Thompson

The Husband's Role
The Wife's Role
Your Passport To Promotion
The Ten Critical Laws of Relationship
The Great Exchange
Give Up Worry Forever
The Endless Pursuit of Excellence
Excellence in Character
Excellence in the Workplace
Excellence in Attitude
Excellence in Ministry
Marriage From God's Perspective
Shattered Dreams
You Are Healed
Victory Over Fear
The Winning Decision

For a complete listing of additional products
by Robb Thompson, please call:

1-877-WIN-LIFE
(1-877-946-5433)

You can also visit us on the web at:

www.winninginlife.org

To contact Robb Thompson,
please write:

Robb Thompson
P. O. Box 558009
Chicago, Illinois 60655

*Please include your prayer requests
and comments when you write.*